The Beginner's Guide
To Pigeon Racing

The Beginner's Guide to Pigeon Racing

S. W. E. BISHOP

*Author of 'The Secret of Eye-Sign'
Ex-Editor of the monthly pigeon
racing journal – Pigeon Racing News
& Gazette.*

PELHAM BOOKS

First published in Great Britain by
PELHAM BOOKS LTD
52 *Bedford Square*
*London W.C.*1
JUNE 1971
SECOND IMPRESSION FEBRUARY 1973
THIRD IMPRESSION NOVEMBER 1975
FOURTH IMPRESSION DECEMBER 1978

© 1971 *by S. W. E. Bishop*

All Rights Reserved. No part of this publication may be reproduced, stored in a retrieval system, or transmitted, in any form or by any means, electronic, mechanical, photocopying, recording or otherwise, without the prior permission of the Copyright owner

ISBN 0 7207 0501 0

Printed and bound in Great Britain by
REDWOOD BURN LIMITED
Trowbridge & Esher

With acknowledgements to 'Old Hand', the Resident Expert of *Pigeon Racing News & Gazette* from whom I have learned a great deal about pigeon racing in my fifty years in the sport. May he long continue to write for your favourite journal.

Contents

Chapter One   THE LOFT   13

The importance of ventilation – choice of materials used in its construction – the loft floor – the Front and Trapping Corridors – ground plan of the loft – the compartments – the sliding doors – trapping the birds – reasons for the provision of a Front Corridor – window shutters – the nestbox design and construction – the facing of the loft – roof lights – installing electricity and plumbing – height of support piers – the anti-pitching roof fence.

Chapter Two   LOFT EQUIPMENT AND ACCESSORIES   29

Perch design – box perch or Big Vee perch? – Nestbox Design – The 'Swinging Door' nestbox – kind of nestbowl – preventing drinkers from icing up in winter.

Chapter Three   PIGEON RACING EQUIPMENT   37

The timing clock – the baskets for training purposes.

Chapter Four   THE FOUNDATION STOCK   39

Buying foundation stock – choosing squeakers, or old birds – changes in types – on prisoners deteriorating in long confinement – the aviary – on ancient strains – how to reduce the odds against starting with sub-standard stock – where to go to buy foundation stock – how to look for faults in racing pigeons – about pedigrees – how to hand-feed young squeakers.

Chapter Five   THE ART OF BREEDING   59

On breeding winners – dedication to the sport – physique and mentality – mating champions together – the 'smash' seasons – nature and conformity – the Fallow Generation – the generations of a family – the 'individual' – Mendel's Law – no equality in parental contribution – the importance of 'vigour' – line-breeding to the Male – study of the eye – racing the squeakers – hardwork and overwork

CONTENTS

– the modern racing pigeon – the 1,000-mile race in 1913 – the rare Producer Hen – serious losses of young hens – the first 'cross' – practical hints – behaviour of birds in the Mating Box – avoid buying already mated pairs – control of the breeders – mating up late-bred birds – the perfection of the egg – testing the fertility of eggs – chilled eggs in the nest – pigeon's milk – the fast growth of nestlings – growth of the plumage – ringing squeakers – 'wet' feeders – culling weaklings – weaning squeakers – teaching squeakers to eat and drink – the appearance of fret-marks – teaching squeakers to use the 'Open Door' method of trapping – the tit-bit.

Chapter Six THE PLUMAGE COLOURS 81

Sex-linkage and its effect on colour-breeding – the Intense Colours and their dilutes – Dominant colours – the Red plumage colours – Recessive colours – Grizzles – the Blue Barred descendants of the Rock Dove – Black velvet – how to harden plumage colour – Whites and Pieds.

Chapter Seven THE DIET 85

Modern racing pigeons need special diets – the vices of grass – Legumes, Cereals and Oil Seeds – the percentages of fat in grain – the critical amounts of vitamins and minerals – the Vitamins – the Tic Bean – Crop-bind – care of the drinking water – the need for salt in the diet – the effect of vitaminic deficiency – the essential minerals – the Carbohydrates – scientifically compounded 'boosts' – grit for racing pigeons.

Chapter Eight TRAINING 99

The disciplines of training – reason for training racing pigeons – the cold East Wind – house-top exercise – teaching pigeons how to fly straight – time to learn – basket-training 'ten-weekers' – the training stages – loss of birds due to aerial clashing – mental attitude and character of racing pigeons – where do lost pigeons finish up? – the dreaded 'Fly-away' – effect of over-crowding the loft – training 'round the loft' – the multiple (repetitive) tossing of young birds and yearlings – controlling youngsters – the effect of the moult – single-tossing yearlings – training old birds – the value of single-up tossing.

CONTENTS

Chapter Nine   PIGEON RACING TECHNIQUES   111

The Natural System and the Widowhood System – rearing a first round of squeakers – mating-up – the bird's manufacture of 'pigeon milk' – staggered matings – racing two-year old birds – racing yearlings – the advantage of 'the jump' – long distance racing – price no criterion of success – the influence of the weather on the race result – the 'smash' race – widowhood cocks – snags in widowhood racing – feeding widowhood cocks – no superior racing systems – the late Fred Shaw and his widowers – deterioration of the hens – the value of the good racing hen – conditions of nest for racing – the after-race care of the bird.

Chapter Ten   THE DRAG   121

The 'nursery' of the sport – the Federations – the Combines – cost of Road Transporters – club radius and federation 'corridor' flying – influence of the wind – wind and weight in the drag – overfly – overfly and the long races – the pilot birds in the drag – the race 'smash' – the effect of the British maritime climate on the racing – the influence of the prevailing wind – North and South Road racing – East wind racing – birds dropping out of the drag – the pilot birds and their work – the Faroe Isles project – the National Smash Race – the 'imaginary' breaking-point – crossing water – channel pigeons – flying solo.

Chapter Eleven   EYE-SIGN   133

Searching for a 'hallmark' – the exception proves the rule – the great importance of the eye to a pigeon – the Eye-Sign classifies visual acuity – the team investigation – Eye-Sign inspections in continental lofts – the coloured Eye-Signs – at Mons. Gobert's loft in Belgium – grading the Gobert pigeons by Eye-Sign – at Cattrysse Bros Loft – the mechanism of the pigeon's eye – the 'Oil-Droplets' – pigment or shadow? – the value of Eye-Sign.

Chapter Twelve   THE MOULT   145

The 'human' moult – the reason why a pigeon moults – the Epidermis, Dermis and Germinal Layers of the skin –

CONTENTS

the keratinzing action – the products of the epidermic cells – the quality of the plumage – the moult and the health of the bird – the 'fret-mark' – the kinds of feather – the order of the moulting of the Primary Flights – the coming of the 'Big Moult' – the ending of the wing moult – food for the moulting period – speeding up the moult – when not to race a moulting bird – storing moulted flights against future need – time to mate to control the moulting process – winter 'down' feather – the fallacy of the 'full' wing.

Chapter Thirteen   AILMENTS AND DISEASES   151

Loft hygiene – respiratory disease – Coccidiosis – Escheria Coli – Polyneuritis – One Eyed Cold – Canker – Pigeon Pox – Plumage Mite – Red Mite – the Depluming Mite – Louse – Moth – Sour Crop – mending a broken leg – Round Worm – test and treatment – danger from cabbages, clover and snails – the wild bird menace – the endless battles with parasites.

Chapter Fourteen   THE RESPIRATORY SYSTEM   159

The difference between human and pigeon respiration – the pigeon's Air Sacs – the 'pneumatic bone' – pigeon's breathing rate, standing and flying – the bird's huge heart – respiration troubles – symptoms – the 'feeders' – the 'aviary' loft.

Chapter Fifteen   THE HEN'S REPRODUCTORY SYSTEM   163

The weaker sex – treatment of the hens – more affectionate – The Ovaries – the Germ Nucleus – the cock must stimulate the hen – the Oviduct – the stages of egg-making – how long does fertilisation last? – period in between the laying of the eggs – incubate only the perfect egg – hatching out double-yolked eggs.

Chapter Sixteen   THE MATHEMATICS OF PIGEON RACING   169

The Great Circle System – pin-pricking the Ordnance Map – Velocity proper – the timing clock – the Clock Station – Flying time – the Master Timer – velocity calculation – the penalty of faking a pigeon timing clock – hours of darkness – testing the timer's running in three positions.

Illustrations

between pages 96 *and* 97

The loft end
Front Corridor
The Trapping Corridor
The loft
The big vee perch
A pigeon nestbowl
The racing pigeon's wing
A feather abnormality
The rump
The racing pigeon's tail
'True descent'
A pigeon racing timing clock
The 'bent' keel
The Rock Dove (*Columba Livea*)
The pigeon's nest
Ringing a squeaker
The growing wing
Hatching of a squeaker
The race ringing

ILLUSTRATIONS

A West Country pigeon show

The eye sign

One eyed cold

Webbed feet

Loading a road transporter

A race liberation

DRAWINGS

A Louvre panel in a loft wall	16
The ground plan of the loft	21
The big Vee perch	30
The nest-bowl	31
The swinging door nestbox design	33
The federation home corridor	123
The eye-sign inspection code	135

I

The Loft

A 'Loft' is the name given to the structure in which we house racing pigeons. We believe the name was coined by the old Belgian fanciers of Liege who actually kept their birds in the lofts (attics) of their homes. However, the continental practice of housing pigeons did not catch on in this country where the vast majority of fanciers preferred to construct separate buildings for their birds and erect them in their back gardens.

When a man toys with the notion of knocking up a back garden loft, what sort of building design does he conjure up in his mind's eye? Inevitably, the traditional garden tool-shed springs into his mind, an oblong, wooden-walled affair with a felted and boarded roof, or one made of corrugated iron, or asbestos, sloping from one long-wall to the other. Unfortunately, the garden-shed type of structure caught on with the result that many pigeon fanciers were seriously handicapped from the outset by the ravages of parasites and diseases of the kind that are inherent in closed lofts of this type, in which insufficient attention is given to ventilation, the suitability of materials used in the construction of the loft, and the evils of over-crowding racing pigeons. Remember, the Belgian fancier's attic loft was spacious, containing much air. No doubt plenty of air constantly blew into his attic from between the tiles.

What is the direct penalty a fancier pays for failing to provide adequate air ventilation in a pigeon loft? The birds contract Respiratory Disease for which there is no medical cure. What disaster occurs in a loft built of unsuitable material? Parasites move in and become residual after which the fancier can never bring his birds into the condition of good health of the winning pigeon. Does over-crowding also inflict penalties? Certainly, because over-crowded old birds are subject to the Stress Syndrome while very young pigeons (in the year of their birth) are driven to stage the tragic exodus known as 'The Fly-Away'.

Most novices buoy up their ambitions on the hope that if they acquire very good (and quite possibly very expensive) stock they will be free to compete on an equal footing with other fanciers. This is not true. A novice with a loft stocked full of potential champions has no future whatsoever unless he houses his birds in a suitable loft structure. The design, as well as the choice of materials, is all important.

Start by getting rid of any idea of building 'a small loft'. Build the biggest and most capacious loft that you can afford and your available garden space will accommodate. My own loft is 93 feet long, 8 feet deep (excluding nestbox space) and I keep in it fewer pigeons than are housed in lofts one third of its size and volume. If I had the space to spare I would increase it to 150 feet or more.

Before starting to build pause and discover what is really meant by the word 'ventilation' because your future as a fancier depends to a very large extent, on what you learn (and put into practice) of this subject.

The word 'ventilation' should not be confused with mere air space. Ventilation implies 'moving air' – air moving at such a speed that it is constantly pushing foul air out of the loft and by rapid exchange keeps the air inside the loft as fresh as that outside of it. Therein lies the great secret of proper air ventilation. The air must move all the time and in such a fashion that it rapidly exchanges itself.

The beginner may ask about the danger of draughts? Of course draughts are dangerous but none can blow into a properly ventilated loft. What is a draught, anyway? It is a stream of cold air playing into a room containing warm air. If the air temperature inside a loft is the same as that outside of it, no draught can be created.

In a structure made of four solid walls and a roof the air cannot possibly be kept moving unless one instals two electrically driven vanes (fans) one drawing in fresh air and one expelling foul air. Unfortunately, I cannot recommend this system because a mechanical breakdown, or a failure in the supply of electric current (such as might be caused by a fuse blowing) might stop the fans from turning for the duration of just one warm summer night with the result that the birds contract respiratory disease before morning.

Let us study the kind of tragedy that occurs in what I term 'a closed loft'. The pigeons stand on perches from where they continually drop excreta onto the floor and exhale a poisonous gas known as Carbon Dioxide. This gas, which is $1\frac{1}{2}$-times heavier than air, tends to fall and build up on the loft floor. All during the night its obnoxious cloud of gas rises upwards and upwards to engulf the pigeons on their perches. Another poisonous gas, known as Ammonium, rises from the pigeons' urine-capped excreta and because it combines freely with Carbon Dioxide the combination produces another but even more obnoxious gas known as Ammonium Carbamate. This gas, now inhaled by all the loft's inmates, irritates and inflames the sensitive membranes that line the birds' respiratory tracts. The result is Respiratory Disease.

Some years ago the staff of *Pigeon Racing News & Gazette* of which I was then Editor, led by its Resident Expert, the famous 'Old Hand', carried out a series of experiments with the object of discovering the very best system of air ventilation for pigeon lofts, based on the moving air principle.

First of all they knocked up a garden-shed type of loft with four solid wooden walls which were then pierced with rows of round holes, $\frac{3}{4}$ inch in diameter. Then – in wind conditions which could be likened to a zephyr – they measured the distance the incoming air current travelled after it had passed into the loft through the round holes. They were disappointed when they found that the incoming air through the round holes flowed only 18 inches after which it became static.

Their next experiment involved the cutting of the rows of holes into slots, each 18 inches long. They were astonished when they found that the air passing in through these slots travelled for a distance of no less than $5\frac{1}{2}$ feet! Here again, the air outside the loft was no stronger than a zephyr. When the slots were fitted with thin boards, fixed at an angle (which converted them to louvres) it was found possible to control the direction of air flow.

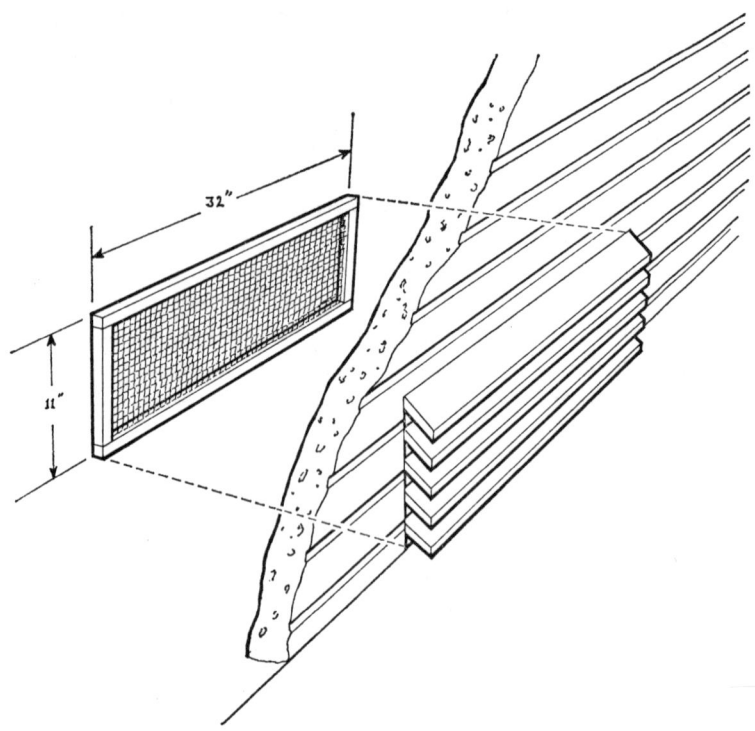

FIG. 1. *A Louvre Panel in a Loft Wall*

The drawing shows the louvre panel (18 inches by 15 inches) inserted in the wall of the loft. Shown separately is the wooden frame, with fine-meshed wire stretched over it which is fixed to the inside wall to cover the louvre panel aperture. Its purpose is to keep vermin out of the loft. If windows with dowels are inserted these, too, should be covered by wooden frames over which fine-mesh wire has been stretched to keep small birds out of the loft

Because inward flowing air should start at floor level, louvre panels of 30 inches wide by 15 inches high were inserted along the loft front just above the floor, extending from end to end of the loft. Another row of panels of equal size were set along the loft front but just below roof level to prevent air from building up in the angle made by front and roof. Finally, a gap not less than 4 inches wide was made to run from end to end of the rear wall where it meets the roof. This allowed the moving air to rise and flow out through this rear-wall gap. Incidentally, they covered this gap with fine mesh wire.

Each end of the loft was then fitted with a large louvre panel, about 3 feet wide and reaching from floor nearly to the roof line. This panel was inserted to face the corridor, not the rear living quarters of the birds (compartments). These end louvres greatly assisted the inward flow of air from the louvres in the loft front. In effect, the loft was given what 'Old Hand' called 'Four-Wall Ventilation' which permitted the air to move through the loft regardless of its direction.

Subsequently, the investigators found that the minimum amount of louvred and vented ventilation requirements in any loft call for a minimum louvred area of 50 per cent of the square area of loft front and both ends, plus the high rear-wall gap. When the ventilation falls below this standard, respiratory disease is inevitable.

What makes a special ventilation system of this kind and magnitude so important to a pigeon loft? Firstly, nature evolved the kind of bird she designed to live and survive in the open air. In fact, the bird we call a 'racing pigeon' is not a pigeon at all! It is the lineal descendant of the Rock Dove which since time immemorial has inhabited the rocky coastline of this country. It lives and nests on exposed rock ledges and unlike so many other species of birds it does not migrate but lives here through all seasons. Nature endowed it with a wonderful plumage which is cold-proof, wind-proof and water-proof.

The racing pigeon (dove) loves the wind (excepting the East Wind which is good for neither man nor beast). When the pigeon flies it never has wind pressing on it at a speed of less than 40 m.p.h. (40 m.p.h. is the racing pigeon's mean speed when flying in conditions of no wind). In favourable winds pigeons have achieved speeds in excess of 100 m.p.h. Now, have you sat on a motor-cycle, or in a car with no windscreen, and exposed yourself to a 40 m.p.h. wind? If not properly clothed you would freeze to death. Racing pigeons thrive in these slip-streams and have been known to fly in them for $17\frac{1}{2}$ hours (all the daylight hours) without dropping down for food or water, or pausing to rest. According to the Beaufort Scale of Wind Forces, a 40 m.p.h. wind is Gale Force Eight yet pigeons thrive when breasting into it for hours and hours on end. Then why keep them cooped up in a closed loft?

The above mentioned expert, 'Old Hand', once knocked a hole (12 inches square) in the wall of his loft and covered it with wire mesh. He then fixed a perch in front of it. His cocks actually fought among themselves for the privilege of roosting on this exposed perch. The pigeon's natural and most favoured environment is the wind (moving air) and it cannot thrive unless it is supplied with a home in which the air is constantly on the move.

So much for air ventilation in pigeon lofts and the novice who ignores what I have written on the subject does so at his own peril – to say nothing of the tragic consequences to his racing pigeons.

Let us now consider the quality of the pigeon's plumage. Birds are in the same category as fur-coated animals in that animals who live in the open air grow better quality fur and feather than animals who live indoors.

It is the plumage that controls the bird's body temperature. Nature gave the pigeon a normal temperature of $107°F$ (against our $98.4°F$) a blood heat which could be lethal to a human being. According to tests made by my staff, pigeons have no difficulty whatsoever in maintaining this very high temperature in arctic conditions (our tests ranged down to $20°$ of frost).

There are other aspects of loft design which call for careful investigation. For example, what happens the moment you install racing pigeons in your new loft? A wide variety of parasites will come from near and far to parasite them. Some of these unwelcome pests will do no more than prevent your birds from enjoying a good night's rest which, in turn, robs them of the energy they need if they are to be given a chance to win a race. Other types of parasite can kill your birds. I refer my reader to the chapter of this book entitled 'Ailments and Diseases'. We pause here to consider how we can make our loft inhospitable to parasites so that they become reluctant to move in and take up permanent residence.

Parasites, without exception, look and hope for a warm, damp loft interior constructed of the kind of material which has a porous surface in which they can burrow and contrive a home from home. Of all the places the most deadly of the parasites likes to patronise, the loft floor is the firm favourite. I refer to the Cocci-worm (Coccidiosis). This wretched invisible worm (invisible to the naked eye) arranges for itself to be swallowed by a pigeon after which it takes up residence in the bird's Small Intestine where it proceeds to kill its host. It can kill in so short a time as 3/4 days. This extremely nasty parasite lives and breeds in damp patches on the loft floor. The enemy of this and a number of other parasites is a floor surface which is hard, waterproof and non-porous and which can be kept as dry as a bone. Another very nasty parasite is the Trichmonais, the Canker germ. This nasty parasite actually explodes when given a dry environment!

Therefore, before we take up tools and start to build we must make up our minds about what type of loft-floor it will be in our best interests to instal. Remember, the yard-stick of your ability as a fancier is your expertise in bringing your birds into that state of physical condition which is known as 'racing form'. Don't handicap yourself from the very outset by putting down the wrong kind of loft-floor.

The finest floor any fancier can instal in his loft is one made of heavy wire-mesh stretched over strong metal frames. The mesh must be very strong because it must support the weight of yourself and any others you take into your loft. The mesh must be no larger than $\frac{1}{2}$ inch to prevent animals getting through it and into the loft.

The floor itself should stand on piers no higher than 12 inches from the ground. Thus, much valuable fresh air can rise in the loft to assist the general ventilation system. The birds' droppings will fall onto the wire-mesh where they will dry out and drop through. I suggest that the ground beneath the loft be covered by a concrete raft whose surface is made to slope gently away so that it carries rain-water away from the under-side of the loft.

Let us suppose that you fail to find a source of supply of a suitable wire-mesh. In any case, whatever else you use for a loft floor it is advisable to protect its underside with ordinary fine wire-mesh to deter animals, such as rats, from eating their way into the loft. Denied the finest loft-floor in the world, you are compelled to find a substitute. I recommend using a chipboard of the 'Weyroc' type (wood chips bonded together by a rock-hard plastic). Alternatively, a floor of the Formica type would be suitable. This floor should not be put down on the piers, with its under-covering of wire mesh, until the tops of the piers have been insulated against rising damp. A sheet of polythene, copper, or slate gives good and lasting insulation.

The above-mentioned materials are free of porosity and are so hard that no parasite that plagues pigeons can find a lodging in them. Further, the material is easy to keep clean, especially if a layer of sand is put down in the pigeons' compartments. The sand prevents the droppings from actually making contact with the surface of the floor and if slaked garden lime is sprinkled over the surface of the sand it helps to accelerate the drying out of the droppings. Any amount of dried out droppings in the loft is harmless to the pigeons, while just one damp dropping is a menace.

In days gone by fanciers used to scrape droppings from wooden or concrete loft floors, as their daily offering to the cause of hygiene but the damp patch left by the scraper provided the best environment for parasites and bacteria to breed in.

Obviously, the floor is of greater importance than the walls and roof. I have no preferences so feel free to choose any material you prefer. If you finish up with a wooden floor cover it with p.v.c. tiles, sheet steel, aluminium or some other damp-proof and non-porous material which is easy to clean. It is easier to clean p.v.c. tiles (using only a mop dipped in 'Flash') than to scrape a wooden floor, in terms of speed and strain, to say nothing of sweat! Remember, if the Cocci-worm gets into your loft floor you can expel it only by charring the entire surface with a blow-lamp.

Why do I labour this point? Because if you ignore it you will have to spend a fortune on anti-parasite specifics, and specifics for the treatment of pigeon ailments and diseases. Do what the sensible pigeon fancier does, and start right.

Now for the design of the loft itself. You are helped to understand my directions by the inclusion of a ground plan drawing and some illustrations. Fig. 2 is the floor plan of the loft, which has been designed to the smallest dimensions I can possibly recommend,

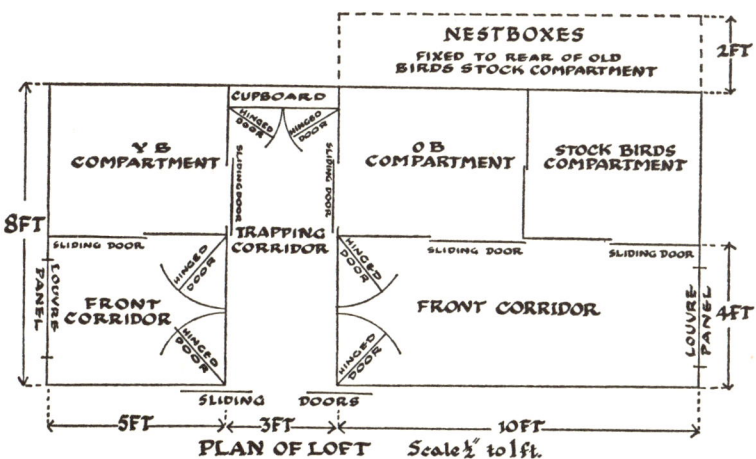

FIG. 2. *The Ground Plan of the Loft*
The plan shows the principal features of the loft design, including the front corridor, the trapping corridor, the three compartments and sliding and hinged door positions

18 feet long, 8 feet deep (front to rear), 7 feet high at the front and 6 feet 6 inches high at rear, with roof sloping front to rear. If you can put up a 28 foot loft please do so but a 48 foot one would be better!

Your attention is next directed to the partitioning of the loft's interior. This is divided up into (1) Corridors, (2) Compartments. Thus, when facing the loft we see first the Front Corridor, running from end to end, and 4 feet wide in front of the compartments. Then, reading from left to right we have first a Compartment, then the Trapping Corridor which is 3 feet wide and runs from front to rear, then on the right of the Trapping Corridor are two more Compartments. All three compartments are 5 feet long and 4 feet deep. They are made by erecting frames covered with fine mesh wire, or closely stationed upright dowels. You will also notice that there are a number of sliding doors in this design and no doubt you may also wonder if all of them are really necessary?

My loft designs, which are only queried by novices, are based on more than fifty years of experience as a pigeon fancier, so every aspect of my loft design has a special meaning and a positive function.

The Corridor which runs from front to rear of the loft is known as 'The Trapping Corridor' because this is the place where your race birds are 'trapped' (caught) when they return from the races. You take them up off this corridor floor to remove the race rubbers you must place in the spools (thimbles) so that they can be clocked. This corridor must not be wider than 3 feet, even if you have plenty of room available. The narrower we make this corridor the easier it will be for you to catch and take up your race birds.

It should be closed by two narrow (18 inches wide) sliding doors. It is advisable for you to build a cupboard at the rear end of the Trapping Corridor, fitted with a shelf. This cupboard accommodates loft cleaning tools, etc., and the shelf carries the timing clock on race day.

At the two points where the Front Corridor crosses the Trapping Corridor it is necessary to station a pair of hinged doors, one set on either side of the Trapping Corridor, as shown in Fig. 2.

Now for the birds' compartments. The one on the left of the Trapping Corridor is the Young Bird Section. The first compartment on the right of the Trapping Corridor is the Old Bird Racing Section and the one on the extreme right is the Stock Loft Section, reserved for producers who are not racing.

Because your young birds (birds in the year of their birth) do not breed, the rear-wall of their section beneath the 4 inch wide ventilation gap is fitted with the Big Vee type of perches. The rear of the Trapping Corridor is, of course, fitted with a cupboard. However, the Walls below the ventilation gap in the two compartments to the right of the Trapping Corridor are not boarded because blocks of nestboxes must be built into these spaces. This nestbox complex is fitted to the outside of the rear wall space of each compartment, so that the whole complex juts out, rearwards, taking up no space inside the birds' compartments. When fixed into position a pitched roof should be mounted above it to carry water away. See illustrations for further detail about nestbox design.

There is a good and sufficient reason for all the sliding doors. It is important to note that the loft is fitted with only one point of access and exit, by the sliding doors that open and close the Trapping Corridor. Why only one entrance and exit? Because for every extra entrance to the loft you would need a Trapping Corridor. This means that on race day one bird would try to pitch in one corridor, and another might choose a second corridor. If this happened you would find yourself trying to break the sprint record chasing first to one and then to another corridor, along the floor of the Front Corridor. What a waste of time and effort? Seconds lost on the clock cost yards in the velocity calculation. The business of catching the bird, taking the rubber race ring from its leg, putting the ring into a spool and then into the timer already adds penalty seconds to your bird's actual flying time so why increase this liability?

In the interests of fast-timing I have provided you with the fastest method of trapping racing pigeons ever invented and perfected. The Open-Door System.

When you wish your birds to trap, show them the customary Seed Tin (get them to know the Seed Tin by always using the same container) then sprinkle a little seed on the floor of the Trapping Corridor. Racing pigeons are inordinately fond of Hempseed. In fact, they crave for it – it is their delight! Keep Hempseed for trapping purposes only, after exercise, training, or racing, get them in with this seed. I suggest a 50-50 mix of Hempseed and Linseed to make an ideal Trapping Mixture.

As the birds pile into the Trapping Corridor after exercise, or as the race bird pitches in, step in behind them and draw the sliding doors together behind your back. The birds are now trapped.

After pecking at the seed the birds will run to left, or right, to regain their own compartment. Now for the inevitable question.

'How will the birds know which way to go to find their own compartment?'

Answer – Because racing pigeons are intelligent they don't often get lost. The best of them knows how to find its way home when tossed 500 miles or more away from home. You may take for granted that the intelligence that brings them home from long distance places also tells them whether they go left or right in the Corridor.

Now and again a pigeon may appear to act stupidly by going to eat or drink in the wrong compartment. This does not mean that the bird is confused, only that it believes – like so many humans – that the water tastes sweeter out of somebody else's tap.

Normally, the birds will use the sliding doors that separate the compartments (you leave them open for them). Alternatively, they can be allowed to use the Front Corridor and regain their compartments through the sliding doors in the Corridor. It is a matter for you to decide. In my loft the birds use the inter-compartment sliding doors while I use the Front Corridor sliding doors when I wish to visit a compartment. This relieves me of the necessity of tramping through compartment after compartment on the Deep Litter and at the same time disturbing the birds in each compartment. Therefore, I let the birds use the inter-compartment doors while I restrict myself to the Front Corridor's sliding doors.

Another question is about to be put to me. Why have a Front Corridor, anyway? I've already given one reason. Here is another. Racing pigeons are very easily panicked. Suppose a cat managed to get into your loft but was caught and removed before it had time or opportunity to attack the birds. The mere sight of the cat inside the loft might cause one or more pigeons to die of shock. The rest would panic. If you let them out to exercise soon after this incident they would fly for a long time and then roost on housetops. You would have the greatest of difficulty in persuading even one or two to trap back into the loft. Most of the birds would spend the night on the house, staring balefully down at the loft where they formerly felt safe but which they now suspect is a trap devised by a cat. Some frightened birds stay out for days, even weeks, while some will clear off and never be seen again.

From time to time a predator will come near to the loft. Cats, the early morning and late evening fox making its rounds of poultry and pigeon places (even in the cities) will try and climb the loft fronts, or stand with front paws gripping the dowels while it eyes a fugitive dinner. But your birds won't panic because between them and the killers stands a dowelled partition, a wide space, and then the loft front.

There is another reason. In certain weather conditions slanting, almost horizontally blown rain and snow might penetrate the louvres to fall on the floor of the Front Corridor. In such an event, none of the moisture will carry far enough to dampen the Deep Litter in the birds' compartments. Therefore, the Front Corridor insulates the rear compartments from moisture.

You will see from the illustration that a row of dowelled windows are fitted in the loft front. Actually, I detest dowels and only use them on this occasion for their ornamental value. Behind the dowels are frames covered with fine mesh wire. This is necessary to keep wild birds out of the loft.

By providing a 4 foot wide Front Corridor we restrict the depth of the birds' compartments to 4 feet, too. Is this a good thing, bearing in mind that the compartment dimension is now 5 feet by 4 feet? Yes, it is a very good thing. Never give pigeons too much room in which to move and manoeuvre. If you stand in the centre of a compartment which is 5 feet by 4 feet you can stretch out your arm and pick up a pigeon wherever it might be perched, or standing, without moving your feet. In a large 8 feet by 5 feet section you would be lucky if you managed to catch the pigeon without a great deal of running and jumping.

Chase a pigeon around the loft and it will panic and because panic is infectious the rest of the birds will also start dashing about, risking injury and damaged plumage. Opt always for small compartments in which you must come into close contact with your birds. This has the effect of making them tame and more docile, therefore easier to catch.

Behind the wire-mesh frame which covers the inside dowelled window I fitted another frame, hinged, which is covered with transparent plastic sheeting. This frame is controlled on its unhinged side by hinged spacers which hold the frame in the open position (held 9 inches away from the wall) from April to October. In this position the window acts like a large louvre. Otherwise, it is only closed from October to April and when the weather is extremely bad.

The number of nestboxes per compartment restrict the number of pairs you can keep in each (eight). Each unit of eight pairs enjoys an air space of 8 feet by 5 feet by, say, 7 feet, or 280 cubic feet of fresh air which is approximately 35 cubic feet per pigeon. The only time when this volume of air is not always available is when there are youngsters in the nest. To the 35 cubic feet mentioned must be added the cubic air capacity of the nestboxes, approximately 5 feet by 7 feet by 2 feet, viz. 70 cubic feet, or approximately another 4 cubic feet per pigeon. An idea of the air space enjoyed by birds in my loft can also be calculated if we multiply the length—93 feet—by the width or depth (10 feet in nine compartments and 8 feet in six) by 7 feet. I keep approximately 60 birds in the loft through the winter and about double that number during 3/4 summer months.

In which direction should a pigeon loft face? The best direction is the driest, South East. Southerly and Westerly directions are subject to most damp conditions. North is hopeless because it has no sun. If you are compelled to build a north-facing loft, arrange for sunlight to enter through rear and roof.

We have yet to discuss the roof and walls of the loft, material-wise. Provided the floor is non-porous I make no hard-and-fast rules about the rest of the structure. If we use non-porous material for walls and roof we are going to be in trouble from condensation which can be as dangerous as the parasites. What I would like to see is just one sheet of corrugated plastic sheeting in the roof over each compartment and over the Trapping Corridor. Never make the roof entirely from transparent material. It would convert the inside of the loft into an unbearable furnace in summer and into a refrigerator in winter. Just one sheet over each compartment is ample.

The Trapping Corridor must be very light. No pigeon will trap into a darkened corridor or loft.

I can still remember the time when in a fit of inspiration I installed electricity in my loft. In the grip of another inspiration I plumbed the loft. I soon found that both installations were boons and a wonderful investment.

Strip lighting was put up along the Front Corridor so that the light shines directly into the compartments. Naturally, the Trapping Corridor is also lit by strip lighting.

'Old Hand' and his helpers carried out experiments on loft decoration. They discovered that nothing equals the splendour and utility of a good white paint. One only needs to ensure that the paint is not lead-based. The better brands serve well. External paintwork needs re-decoration every second year but the loft interior should be renewed at least once a year.

Creosote will not keep parasites out of the loft for long and nothing looks worse than a dismal, drab interior. My advice is to lay in a store of anti-parasite powders and use them regularly. I also recommend you to cover the louvre apertures with fine-mesh wire stretched over frames. Better be safe than sorry!

Allow no wild birds access to your loft. Sparrows bring 'roup' diseases. Starlings bring in the Itch (Depluming) Mite. Jays will steal the eggs from the nests of your birds.

Earlier I said the loft should stand on 12 inch piers. There is a reason. Lofts that stand higher off the ground need a short ladder, or some steps, so that one can mount to enter. These steps can be slippery and dangerous in wet weather. If the loft floor is only 12 inches above ground level one can easily step into it.

Pigeons should never be allowed to pitch onto house, or loft, roof. Keep them off the loft by erecting 18 inch posts at intervals along the edge of the roof. Then thread strands of plasticised wire through the posts, each strand 6 inches apart. This will stop birds using the loft roof. They must pitch straight from the air into the trapping corridor, every time. It will be seen that the modern pigeon loft is not just a shed but a highly functional structure containing many devices which contribute to the health of its inmates and the better enjoyment of our great sport.

II

Loft Equipment and Accessories

The very first loft accessory that comes to mind is the perch. No racing pigeon can be happy in a loft unless it has a perch to roost on. It prizes its perch so highly that it will fight desperately to retain possession of it. Therefore, make sure that the Young Bird compartment is fitted with more perches than are needed to accommodate all the young pigeons. You will notice that the cocks seize the highest perches, making the hens accept the lowest. There is no chivalry between the sexes.

What design of perch is the best to make and instal? Apart from the fancy-perches designed by a few fanciers the most popular are (1) The Box-Perch, (2) The Vee-Perch.

The box perch, as its name implies, is a box nailed to a loft wall, open at the front. When making these perches fanciers use two long planks of timber about $\frac{3}{4}$ inch thick and divide them by fitting vertical pieces of the same planking at roughly 10 inches apart and 10 inches high. The result is a row of boxes, one for each bird to stand in.

The 'Vee-Perch' is also the shape of its name in the form of an inverted 'V'. The bird grips and stands on the crest of the 'Vee'. The modern type is referred to as the 'Big-Vee' because the two pieces of material that are fixed together at right angles are each 12 inches long and six inches wide.

Now let us compare the advantages and disadvantages of the two types of perch. In the Box Perch the pigeon must stand for considerable periods of time in its own excreta. This is not hygienic.

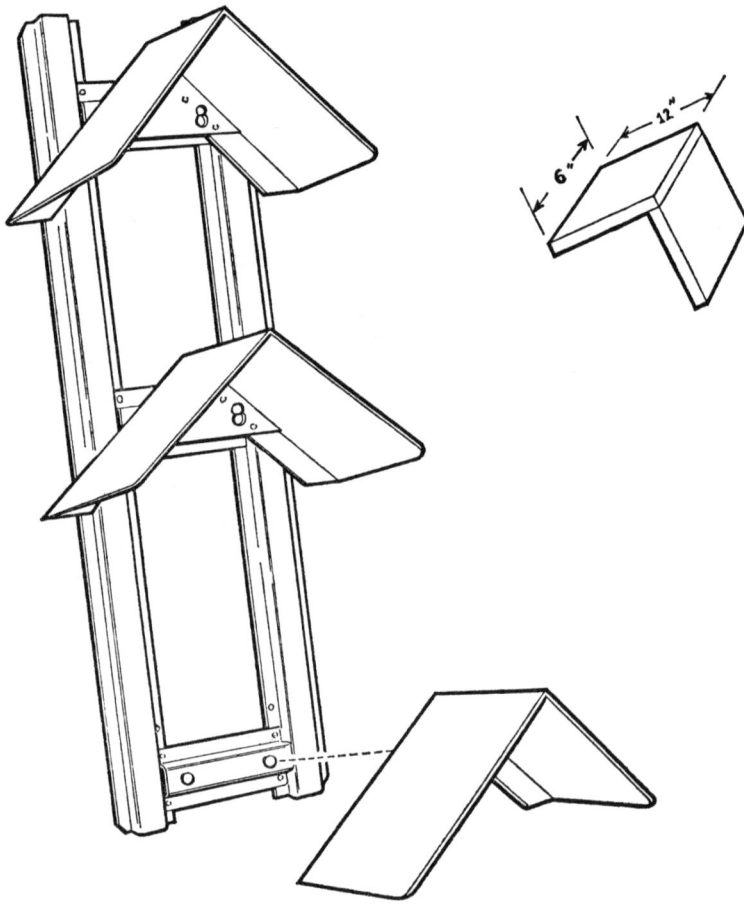

FIG. 3. *The Big Vee Perch*
On the left of the illustration the plastic big vee perches are shown carried on the wall-fitting bracket. Up on the right is shown the method of making home-made big vees with actual sizes of timbers cut

Further, when it sits down at night, also nestling into its own excreta, it tends to thrust its closed wings upwards, into a corner of the box-perch. This can and often does lead to the damaging of the primary flights, often causing them to grow curved instead of straight. One further defect of the box-perch is that it contributes to constant fighting with consequent damage to plumage and eyes.

The 'Big-Vee' type of perch has none of the disadvantages of the Box-Perch. If 'Big-Vee' perches are mounted one above the other, at 12 inch to 14 inch spacing, no perched pigeon can see another so its urge to fight is not sparked off. Its droppings will run down either of the steep sides of the perch and will not foul the birds sitting below, whereas the Box Perch offers no protection against plumage fouling.

Further, no birds can fight on the steep slopes of the perch. Box-perches are not easily constructed by the amateur but anyone can knock up the Big-Vee type. Here again, chipboard bonded with plastic is by far the best material.

We must now give our attention to nestbox design. Already constructed and fitted to the rear wall space, where they give the impression of bookshelves, they obviously need to be fitted with the necessary 'front' and other components. Visits to pigeon lofts in the district will reveal diversity of nestbox front design but after fifty years of pigeon keeping during which I experimented with a number of different designs I came to the conclusion that there is only one really effective design and this one I refer to as 'The Swing-Door' type.

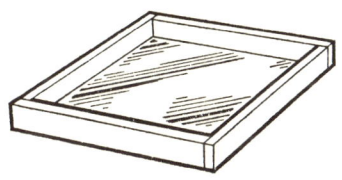

FIG. 4. *The Nest-Bowl*

Shows a simple, home-made nestbowl, constructed from four pieces of wood batten 1½ inches wide by 9 inches long. The bottom of the 'nest-bowl' can be made from three-ply, linoleum, perforated zinc sheeting, aluminium sheet or plastic sheeting

In effect you have a nestbox space of some 30 inches by 18 inches deep by 15 inches high. There are eight of these spaces in the nestbox complex. We now have to turn these shelf-spaces into proper nestboxes by first fitting a dowelled partition which separates the nestbox into two compartments. Note, please, that this partition starts some 5 inches inside the box (from the front edge). Therefore, it does not part-off the whole depth of the box. Two more dowelled frames are attached to the nestbox front leaving a central space between them of some 6 inches. We now attach a Vee perch, much smaller than the wall-fitting type, to the entrance to the box and by means of a hinge. Thus, when the perch is down it provides a small platform onto which the bird can land before entering the box but when lifted up and secured with a bolt or button-catch it can close the nestbox entirely. Finally, we attach a 'swing' door to the partition wall of the nestbox so that it can swing to left and right to close the compartment on either side. We attach hasp and clasp to the door and the two fronts to the box so that when swung to either side the door can be locked in position.

The design has now provided us with a centrally-divided nestbox with two compartments which can be closed either to left or right, to our choice. Let me explain my reasons behind this design. Firstly, we have presented ourselves with a 'Mating-Up Box'. When introducing a cock to a new hen we must go about the task carefully. For example, if we were to lock a pair of birds in a box in the expectation that they would automatically 'take to each other' and mate we might be very disappointed. No cock likes to be separated from his hen, or be under compulsion to accept a new one. Once mated, a pair of pigeons stay mated until the death of either one of the pair. This is their nature. But if for purposes of pedigree we wish to 'break up' an existing mating and re-mate the cock and hen to new mates we must first separate the sexes for a reasonable amount of time (say, seven weeks, or perhaps months) and then arrange for the new proposed matings to be carried out very carefully. If we brought cock and new hen together it is more than likely that the cock would try and savage the hen.

We do not put the cock and hen in a box and hope they will soon mate up. Instead, we use a 'Mating Box' which has a dowelled

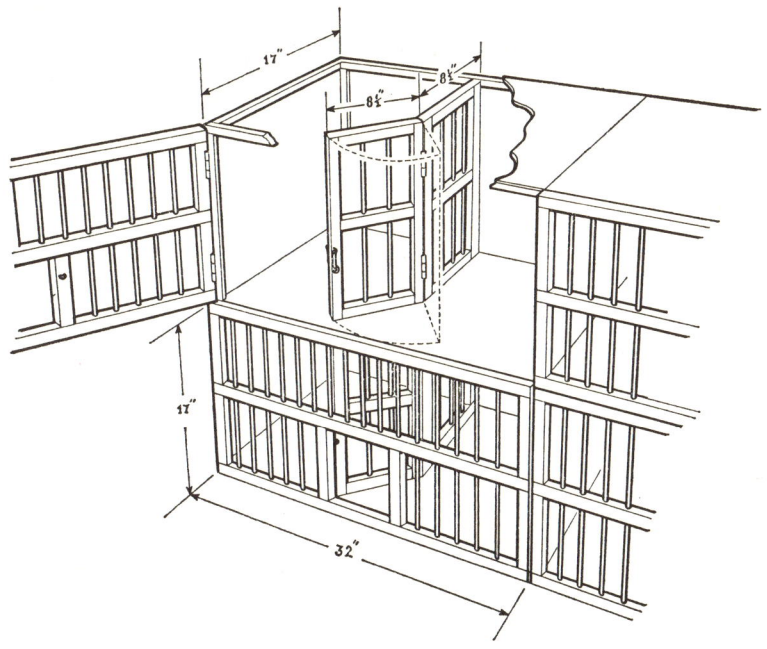

FIG. 5. *The Swinging Door Nestbox Design*
Shows the general design of the swinging-door type of nestbox. The entrance to the nestbox is fitted with a hinged vee (smaller edition of the 'big vee') which when in the open position (hanging down) provides a landing board for the pigeon on which to enter and leave the nestbox. When raised, to close the nestbox, its angle piece assumes the horizontal line and provides the bird with a perch on the outside of its nestbox. The landing board-cum-perch is not shown in this drawing

partition dividing it into two compartments, a hinged door leading to each. We place the cock in one side and the hen in the other and lock them in. If you have built the 'Swinging Door' type of nestbox, you have a 'Mating Box' already at hand. Put the hen in one side and lock the 'swinging door'. It is not necessary to lock the cock in his side provided he has already taken possession of the box as his own. It is a mistake to leave his old hen in his compartment, or anywhere where he can see or hear her.

No one can put a period on the length of time it will take a strange cock and hen to mate. Some cocks and some hens are more stubborn than others but only in exceptional cases will the cock waste more than four days in sulking and hating the hen you have imprisoned in his nestbox. If you make periodical visits to the loft and study the birds you are trying to mate up you will notice that eventually the two birds start to nod to each other and they will then try to caress through the dowelling. When this behaviour is noted take out the hen and lock the compartment she has been occupying. She may now cohabitate with the cock in the other compartment of the box. Thus, you benefit from the first utility virtue of the 'Swinging Door Nestbox'.

Its second virtue will be swiftly appreciated when the youngsters in the nest of the first round reach the age of approximately 14 days. They are now fully feathered and very demanding of food from both sire and dam. This upsets the hen because at this stage the cock again 'starts to look at her' with another round of eggs in mind. Unfortunately, every time she tries to get into the nestbowl with her mate and go through the motions which are the preliminaries of all matings the youngsters will pester her for food and keep squeaking.

In order to get away from her youngsters the hen will try and find another nestbox and if no spare ones are available she will try and tempt her mate into fighting another cock for his box with the result that the peace of the loft will be destroyed.

The moment you see the cock 'looking at his hen again' unhasp the Swinging Door and pull it across to the next compartment. This action will imprison the youngsters in their compartment so that the hen will be free to enter the compartment which has been locked up, up till now. What about food for the youngsters by the first round? Nothing could be better because the parents will continue to feed their youngsters through the dowelled partition but the youngsters cannot pester their mother any more. If you stand a pot of water and corn in the hen's side but up against the dowelled box partition the youngsters can watch sire

LOFT EQUIPMENT AND ACCESSORIES

and dam feeding and drinking and quickly learn how to fend for themselves.

If the youngsters are locked in the nestbox compartment and a fight starts in the adjoining compartment they will escape the trouble. Unfortunately, when a fight starts in the average nestbox the youngsters are stamped flat by the fighting cocks. Here again, the 'Swinging Door' type of nestbox pays off.

It is possible that as the years pass you may feel tempted to try out 'The Widowhood System' of racing. I will not go into detail of this system here because I am dealing with it in another chapter, except to point out that under this 'celibacy' system the fancier must be able to imprison the hen in the cock's nestbox so that he may see her, even caress her but make no physical contact of a sexual nature. The 'Swinging Door Design' adapts perfectly to this requirement. Thus, by adopting my design of nestbox the beginner is granted three very important functions which will gratify him in the years to come.

A refinement of the design would be the attachment of a transparent plastic box to each of the nestbox's two dowelled fronts in which you could stand pots for food and water.

Another item of loft equipment is the 'nestbowl'. This is the actual nesting unit which has been available for centuries in the form of an earthenware bowl with steep sloping sides. Frankly, I detest them. If a nestling falls out of the bowl when it is not feathered, or only partly feathered, it will freeze to death. It has no chance of climbing back into the bowl.

Remember, the unfeathered youngster is still a reptile. It does not become a warm-blooded mammal until it is feathered.

My 'nestbowls' consist of four pieces of wood about 9 inches long and $1\frac{1}{4}$ inches high by $\frac{3}{4}$ inch thick fitted together to form a square frame. There is no need to fit bottoms to these square frames. Just stand them on 21 sheets of paper torn from newspapers, or old journals. Then, each day from hatching, one only needs to lift the square frame and by removing the top layer of paper also take away the droppings, replacing the frame on a perfectly clean sheet of paper. If a youngster gets out of this frame it can climb back in again with ease.

Drinking water must be made available to birds in each section.

My practice is to place metal troughs in the Front Corridor but up against the dowelling so that the pigeons can push their heads through the gaps between the dowels and drink, the dowelling prevents them from fouling up the water.

Food is placed in hoppers which are also stood against the dowelling, beside the drinkers.

The drinkers must not only be emptied but actually scrubbed out three times a day in the summer months. In lofts where no electricity is available water can be stopped from freezing in drinkers by standing a small jam jar in the water (so that no water can get into the jar) and lighting a night candle in it. The warmth will stop the water from icing over. With electricity available one can insert an aquarium heater controlled by a thermostat which cuts in the heater when the temperature drops to a low level. I suggest setting the thermostat at about 35°F.

Pigeons suffer if they cannot drink at regular intervals. Once a day, when the ice is broken for them, is not enough.

III

Racing Equipment

A beginner needs items other than loft accessories before he can race pigeons. His first move should be to find out the name and address of the secretary of the local pigeon racing club. A letter to the secretary of the Homing Union should bring the desired information if a stamped addressed envelope is enclosed. The moment the beginner is accepted as a club member he automatically becomes a member of the Union and should receive a Rule Book. I advise the beginner to study the Rule Book.

The big union that governs the sport in England (other than the North East) is The Royal National Homing Union, The Reddings, Cheltenham, Gloucester. The North of England Homing Union governs Durham, Northumberland and North Yorks. Scotland, Wales and Northern Ireland have their own Unions.

Your greatest need is for a pigeon timer. This is a very special timing clock which was specially designed for the use of pigeon fanciers. It is an expensive item of equipment as well as being a necessary one and you are advised to buy the best model you can get. Don't haggle over the price, even if it frightens you! Cheap second-hand timing clocks are never really cheap but expensive in the long term. They usually develop the sort of trouble that costs you dearly. For instance, in what kind of temper would you be if after clocking a winning pigeon you are disqualified because your timer stopped running, or recorded an incorrect time? One can be penny-wise and pound-foolish.

The modern timer is a continuously running 8-day time clock

which prints the time on a roll of paper, recording Days, Hours, Minutes and Seconds. Do not show any interest in secondhand ancient timers that record the time by puncturing a hole in a printed clock dial, or dials. Most of these old timers record only to the nearest five seconds. Of what use is this time recording when the first ten birds in a federation race are clocked well within ten seconds? Had you competed in such a race and clocked in the second lot of five your bird could have been unplaced.

Fortunately, pigeon timers are usually so well made that the one you buy should last a lifetime and beyond. Take care of it by having it cleaned and oiled every year. The club retains your timer during the racing season and it is handed to you in a sealed condition on the eve of a race but it is returned to your possession in the closed season.

Don't leave the timer in your loft where damp can be as big an enemy as it is to your pigeons. Take it into the house and store it in a very dry room.

Most fanciers like to train their own pigeons. This means that you need training baskets or crates. I advise you to train your own birds if you own or have access to the necessary transport, such as your own motor cycle, or car! I always thoroughly enjoy this chore. The cheaper sort of training basket is made of willow and enjoys a short life which can be extended if the baskets are re-varnished every year. A very nice training basket made of plastic is also available and it has the merit of not spraying chips and sawdust in cars. It should also last several lifetimes but it costs more than the willow basket.

The thimbles or spools used with the timers are not universal but vary in size and design according to which timer they are made to fit. I advise you to acquire a dozen of these thimbles because for a reason I have never fathomed they are constantly getting lost.

IV

The Foundation Stock

As an intelligent person you will have studied the first three chapters of this book and resisted any temptation to acquire Foundation Stock until your loft has been designed and built. Only now, with a first-class loft waiting to receive its first inmates, do you allow your mind to concern itself with the project of buying some foundation birds.

You will notice that I referred to 'buying' your stock because this is the operative word. I know it is difficult for any of us to look a gift horse in the mouth but I assure you that the very worst way of starting your career as a pigeon fancier is by allowing someone, even a friend, to press gift pigeons onto you. I hope I offend no one, especially those honest chaps who, like myself, would never dream of letting an inferior bird pass from their lofts into another, when I suggest that in most cases, fanciers who are anxious to give pigeons away wish to be rid of the specimens they do not care to cull. Instead of suppressing them, or sending them to a poulterer, they hand them to some poor novice who in the years to come is to wonder why he is getting nowhere with the blood of the gift-making Ace. The fact is that Aces, like all other fanciers, also breed some rubbish during the season.

Ask yourself if you would give away pigeons of great value, or even of any real worth? No matter how choice is one's stock, only a mere handful of birds survive a season's breeding to rank as consistent long distance racers, far too few to permit the deduction of 'gifts'. My second warning to the beginner is to stay away from dealers. Like all sports, we have them, people who make comfortable livings by flogging pigeons to all and sundry and often in a wholesale manner. Naturally, they insist that every bird they sell is a potential champion but please try and resist the urge to buy from them.

Study the Fancy Press and sort out the names of two or three fanciers whose sterling performances impress you and from whom you think you would like to acquire some stock. Write to all three and make appointments to call and see them and their birds. In that way you will learn much and may even make at least another new friend in the sport. Pigeon fanciers are the most friendly of men (except when some of them attend general meetings) and the more of them you meet the more will you appreciate why pigeon racing is the best sport in the world.

When you are looking round for Foundation Stock two choices are open to you. Do you start with squeakers, or with old birds? Let us investigate both projects.

If you buy squeakers of 24 days old, you should have no difficulty whatsoever in settling them in your loft and have them flying out every day. If the squeakers are older than 24 days when they reach you and are wing-strong (can fly up to a perch) you might be unlucky when trying to settle them. Always make clear to the fancier from whom you are buying the youngsters that they must be only 24 days old on the day they reach you, otherwise they will be sent back. Squeakers installed at this tender age should adopt your loft with alacrity and they could even be raced to it that season (1st August onwards) if you so desired.

If you acquire old birds you are not entitled to believe that they, too, will be settled with ease and in a very short time be flown out from the loft. I know pigeons vary in temperament. One can be lucky and settle an old bird in a few weeks at first time of asking. On the other hand, an old bird can be obstinate and insist on trying to work his way back to his old loft. I know which type I prefer. Therefore, if your need is for birds that can be settled without tears, and be flown round the chimney pots in a matter of days, your best bet is to install squeakers. Now ask yourself if the settling of the birds is the only criterion that should be applied to your selection of Foundation Stock?

It most decidedly is not! No fancier, living or dead, ever looked at a 24-day-old squeaker and with certainty predicted that, 'This one will definitely be a winner.' You can never tell with squeakers. Buying them is an all-out gamble, the biggest a fancier can ever take. You could go to a loft, and a winning one, too, and if the owner agreed, select a dozen youngsters from the best nests but the odds against you selecting just one long distance winner of the future would be at least 25 to 1. This accounts for the reason why squeakers cost less than old birds.

What about buying old birds instead of squeakers? Are their qualities easier to appraise and evaluate? The answer is – Yes! In any case, you could couple your offer for the old bird with the proviso that the bird must have a proven history of performance behind it. An expert could most certainly study the bird on offer and tell you if the bird had a chance to breed anything useful.

Pigeon racing is a sport that differs very much from the other two great livestock sports, horse-racing and greyhound racing because a pigeon fancier is required to breed his own champions. This means that he not only manages and trains his pigeons, he must also be their breeder, a dual responsibility that would shake the racehorse and greyhound fraternities to their socks. As any novice soon discovers, being a manager and trainer of racing pigeons is child's play compared to the work of breeeding one's own champions.

One must know how to match class with class to produce a long distance type. It does not necessarily follow that the progeny you breed down from your original Foundation Stock will in its turn breed birds of the same type. It is claimed that 'Like Breeds Like' but whenever I let birds go to another loft three or four generations later their descendants look very unlike the originals.

This change in type occurs for two very good reasons. Firstly, Mother Nature never allows any living thing faithfully to reproduce itself. There must be a difference in phenotype of some kind. Secondly, few fanciers will go to the trouble of ousting all diversions from type. No fancier should keep and breed from a bird whose general conformity is at variance, even slightly, with the family type because it isn't possible for any fancier to preserve a 'type' if he breeds from a bird or birds who portray a departure from the accepted pattern, say, by acquiring greater or smaller size, longer necks or legs, deeper or shorter keels, and so on. If you cull your variants and breed always to a type you will always know where you stand. Allow non-conformity to breed in your loft and you never do.

There are a wide diversity of types in the lofts. There is the sort of pigeon that wins an occasional prize or pool in club races but rarely, if ever, in Federation events. I refer to this type as 'the good club pigeon'. Much fun can be had with this type of pigeon if the owner is not ambitious to shine in classic racing. We also have the type of bird that is fairly reliable up to 350 miles but which fails regularly at long distances. The 500/600 mile winner in Open events is a much rarer bird, in a class of its own.

The salient fact about old bird prisoners (old birds who cannot be flown out of the loft because they would clear off if given the chance) is that pigeons, like men, deteriorate if they are kept in long confinement. I detest keeping old bird prisoners. It is only my irresistible itch to acquire an occasional notable champion that lumbers me with old bird prisoners. My dislike for housing them is not based on any sentimental reason but on my experiences as a fancier which tells me that youngsters bred from captive parents never seem to possess the vitality and vigour of the progeny of birds who are freely flying out of the loft. I discovered that the only way to breed good, robust youngsters from old birds after their first year of imprisonment in the loft was to provide them with an aviary for use during the day. There is no set size for an aviary except that I advise you to provide yourself with the largest that space will allow. This aviary should adjoin the loft and access to it should be through a small, hinged door from the loft itself. The provisos are that the aviary shall be all fine-wire mesh covering three sides, the roof and – note specially – the floor which should be at least 12 inches above ground level.

If you permit the aviary to use an earth floor much trouble might result. I want the birds' droppings to fall onto the wire mesh floor where they may dry and drop through to the earth below where they can be scraped away regularly and be deposited on the garden compost heap. My present aviary is 10 feet long, 5 feet

6 inches high and 4 feet wide, fixed to the left hand side of my loft. Naturally, only a mere handful of birds use it (I should need a much larger aviary if I kept more than three or four pairs of prisoners). Provide some perches for the birds so that they can sit out in the aviary, stretch their wings, get some sun on their backs and plenty of fresh air. Don't forget to give them the regular use of the bath. When nesting time comes along deposit goodly supplies of suitable twigs in the aviary so that the birds can make their own nests. Incidentally, I have never lost a bird when settling provided it had at least one season in the aviary. I reiterate that an aviary is a vital requisite for the continuing good health of prisoner stock.

Types of pigeons are fixed by 'strain', another name for 'family'. Even so, I feel obliged to warn my reader against recognising and using ancient strain names. The Gits, Grooters, Gurnays, Delmottes, Jurions, Soffles, Hansennes, Jannsens and Wegges, like the Delrez, Lamottes, and many others whose names we often hear repeated today, disappeared many years ago. The men who made those strains famous died a long, long time ago. On their deaths their teams were disbanded and subsequently passed into other lofts. Most of those ancient 'greats' died last century or, like the great N. Barker, at the beginning of this century. Any comparison with the stock they bred and cultivated for themselves and that claimed by some modern fanciers as being identical to those ancient strains would be purely coincidental. Forget the ancient strain names, including the Stanhopes, Lulhams and other noted but ancient British strains, such as the famous Logans. I owned birds of the Logan strain at a time when the great J. W. Logan was still alive and racing. Today I prefer to refer to my old family as the Bishop-Logans to indicate that while my family had its roots in the Old Logan Blood (of which there were none better) I have used my own 'crosses' so that the strain is no longer Logan but Bishop-Logan.

I once asked a very successful racehorse trainer how he went about selecting yearling horses (unraced and untrained) for his clients when he attended Yearling Bloodstock Auction sales. On what did he base his judgment?

'Well,' he replied, 'you've got to know something about horseflesh when you inspect a possible purchase. But no one could tell with certainty whether a yearling is likely to be a winner or an also-ran, just by inspecting it. My method is simple and it nearly always succeeds. I won't buy a yearling unless I've checked up on its parents and discovered that both its sire and its dam have bred a winner or two.'

I pass this piece of advice to the beginner because I think it is worth a great deal of money. Those fanciers who applied the same principle to their selection of racing pigeons could do much worse.

When reading pigeon journals you will be inundated with advice which probably includes the hoary, 'Go to a successful loft in your locality and there buy your foundation stock.' Like a lot of other pigeon racing advice this suggestion should also be left strictly alone. Is the local Ace likely to relish the prospect of starting up a potentially keen rival with the best of his bloodstock, on his very doorstep, so to speak? In my long experience of pigeon racing I have found very few Santa Claus, especially among local Aces. The beginner would do better if he went further afield and acquired stock from an Ace with whom he is unlikely to engage in direct competition.

Big winning pigeons do not usually breed exceptional winners of their own calibre, that is, if they breed any winners at all. I've known fanciers who paid very high prices for pigeons (I plead guilty of the same action) and failed to breed anything but rubbish from them. I don't know the reason why hard-raced hens do not appear to be the best and most reliable of producers and in my time I've owned not a few but a great many champion long distance racing hens. A good hiding in the races seems to deprive them of their powers of reproducing champion stock. Hard work does not appear to deprive racing cocks of their powers although I have known over-raced cocks to become sterile.

Suppose you decide to acquire old birds for your Foundation Stock and thereby avoid much of the huge gamble of making a start with squeakers, how will you know that the fancier who supplied you with stock has not sold you a pigeon in a poke? How can you, a mere beginner, tell a good pigeon from a poor or bad one? While I cannot hope to convert you into a learned selector

THE FOUNDATION STOCK

of 'crack' pigeons through this printed advice I can, at least, tell you what kind of pigeon to avoid. Read on.

Make an appointment with the fancier of your choice and accept his invitation to enter his loft and inspect his birds. Anticipating your call, the fancier will have cleaned out and tidied up his loft, making it look as attractive as possible. The vast majority of fanciers are 'house-proud' and hate anyone to find them with a dirty loft so expect to find a clean one. If the loft is filthy you can always shorten your polite visit and get out of it. Incidentally, if you call on a strange fancier without having first made an appointment (an oversight and breach of good manners) he will probably keep you waiting in his house while he slips out to his loft and gives it the once over.

When you enter his loft take careful note of the condition of the droppings. If he cleaned out recently few droppings will be in evidence but during your stay keep your eyes peeled. If the droppings, or some of them, are not firm and round, white-capped by urine, but are loose and sloppy, suspect that there is ailment in the loft and that it would be very foolish for you to acquire stock from it in case you transport the bacteria to your own loft. Listen, too, for sneezing, coughing and rattling by a bird or birds, a sure sign of respiratory disease in the loft. Be quick to notice if any of the birds are hunched-up, feathers blown and looking miserable. I know that a wise fancier would whip any such birds out of the loft and hide them away before you were allowed to enter the place but some forget to do this.

No matter whose loft you visit you will be expected to handle some birds so waste no time in getting to know the 'feel' of a good, bad, or indifferent pigeon.

Don't imagine that a pigeon is made of glass and marked 'fragile'. The bird won't shatter in your hands. Racing pigeons are physically tough and although they must be handled gently there is no need for you to feel anxious about holding one in your hand.

If the bird is perched and you wish to take it up, show it one hand and take it up with the other. All pigeons fall for this trick. It rarely fails. Take up the bird by bringing your open hand down on its back. Never try to take up a pigeon by placing your hand under its body and never, never try to catch a bird who is standing with its back to you. You might pull its tail out.

Let the bird lie in your hand with its beak pointing towards your chest so that it is really cupped in your hand with your thumb reaching up and over to press down firmly but gently on its back. Make your thumb grip a firm one, or the bird may struggle in your hand and lose feathers from its back. Its two legs should be gripped between your first and second, or second and third, fingers. Now the bird can relax in your hand and be comfortable. You may now carry out your inspection of the bird.

First of all let your fingers on the underside of the bird's breast-bone (Sternum Bone) otherwise known to fanciers as 'the keel', feel along the length of this bone. Is the bone dead straight? Or do your fingers detect a bend or wave in the bone? If you find the bone bends or waves the bird contracted what we call 'a bent keel'. The accident that distorted and malformed this bone occurred when the bird was hatching from the egg and it indicates a skeletal weakness. This defect doesn't necessarily condemn the bird because many birds with this defect have won races but you are looking for 'perfect' specimens so make sure you get them.

Now feel the bird's claws (feet). Are they warm, or cold? If the latter politely inform the fancier that you would like to see another bird. Birds who are cold in their extremities usually suffer from poor circulation of the blood. The condition also indicates that perhaps the heart is undersize. If the claws are cold, hand the bird back to the fancier and ask to see another.

Now take the root of the outside feather of the wing between the thumb and index finger of your disengaged hand and pull it away from the bird. This action should cause the wing to open, fanwise. This is called 'spanning the wing'. You should now be able to count the feathers which we call the Primary Flights. There are ten of them and each is numbered from 1 to 10 starting with No. 1 which is the inside flight of the wing counting from the Secondaries outwards to No. 10 which is also referred to as 'The Pinion Flight'. Inspect each one of the ten primary flights, looking for a tiny indentation, or crease, across the quill of the flight (the quill is the main stem of the feather out of which the broad webbing (or vane) grows. If the bird has been worked the 'fret-

THE FOUNDATION STOCK 47

mark' (crease) you find across the quill was probably contracted when the bird spent a night out in a race. This 'fret-mark' does not condemn the bird but it is a good reason for you to ask the fancier how the fret-mark was caused.

The ten feathers of the wing which grow next to the Primary Flights are known as the Secondaries and you will see that they are of a different shape from the Primaries. In the aerodynamic sense the Primaries are known as the work-flights while the Secondaries, which also work, are better known for 'the lift' they give to the wing.

In a good racing pigeon there should be an appreciable step between the length of the last Secondary and its adjoining feather, the first Primary flight. This 'step' is known on the continent as 'decalage'. The 'step' should measure $\frac{3}{8}$ to $\frac{1}{2}$ inch. If you find no 'step' at all let your interest in the bird immediately evaporate.

The bones in the pigeon's wing equate to a large extent with the animal's normal front legs. The upper arm bone (the Humerus) is known as the Pneumatic Bone because it contains no marrow, only an air sac. This means that if this particular bone breaks its lack of marrow will prevent it from mending. Now, the length of this upper arm bone must be no longer than the distance between the centre line of your thumb's joint and its tip. If you don't trust your thumb as a yardstick note that the length of the bone must not exceed $1\frac{3}{8}$ inches. Always make sure to measure this upper arm bone and lose interest in any bird whose bone is longer than the measurement I have given you. The reason for this precaution is in the leverage calculation which I will not explain just now.

Return to the bird's keel. Does the keel sweep sweetly, in a gentle curve, from the bird's chest to its stomach? The end of this bone should lie not far from the vent bones which you can find easily because the two thin bones lie side by side just under the root of the tail feathers. The upward sweep of the keel must correspond closely to the shape of a boat's keel which curves up to the aft or stern end. If the keel is short and straight, and somewhat sharp of edge, reject the pigeon.

Now feel the Great Pectoral Muscles. One of each lies along either side of the Keel. These are the work muscles of flight. The skinny Lesser Pectoral you won't feel but your fingers are free to explore the Great Pectoral muscles which give the bird its power and speed in the air. Muscle is all important to a racing pigeon which is, in fact, the most muscular animal in the world. No less than forty-per-cent of its body weight should be devoted to muscle of which total the Greater Pectoral Muscles should equal 50 per cent. If the bird is deficient in muscle discard it.

The Great Pectoral Muscle must be so plumped up as to actually bulge on either side of the keel and to such an extent that when the bird is viewed at the front its body appears to be ovate in shape, rather than round. A pigeon is badly muscled when it appears to possess what is known as 'a deep keel'. The skeletal difference between a 'shallow' and a 'deep' keel is only $\frac{1}{8}$ inches so the word is a misnomer. The real contributory factor to what we call 'a deep keel' is paucity of muscle. So, the 'deep-keeled' bird will have a Vee-shaped body with steep sides sloping down to a prominent, sharp keel. Here again, if you find yourself handling this kind of pigeon hint that you are ready to transfer your interest to another specimen.

Now transfer your inspection to the bird's rump. You will find this on its back at the place where the tail feathers sprout and where your thumb is probably pressing down. The bird's back should be slightly arched and hard. When your thumb presses down in the region of the rump its pressure should be resisted. If the thumb sinks down into a recess or pit it is because the feather at the root of the tail is too sparse. Do not forgive this inadequacy.

While inspecting the Rump, let your eyes wander to the bird's tail. Now twist your wrist a little, tilting the bird forward then backwards. Does the bird's tail come shooting up, like a periscope, or does it tend to drop down? If the latter, carry on with your inspection but if the former tell its owner, in as nice a tone of voice as you can muster, that the bird in your hand may have good points but that it isn't the one you are looking for.

Now take the bird into both hands, palms below the bird to release the thumb and forefinger of both hands, so that they are free to grip the root of both outside tail feathers (known as the Tail Rectrices). Pull on these two feather roots and the tail feathers should open just like a lady's fan. This is called 'Fanning the Tail'.

THE FOUNDATION STOCK 49

The tail should contain twelve rectrices or, rather, six pairs. The feathers that cover the root of the tail and the outside of the wings are known as the 'Coverts'. If your inspection of the Rectrices should reveal a discoloration of the quill of one of the feathers, known as 'a white streak', which is upwards of an inch long (not the outside white margin on the two outside tail feathers of the Blue Chequer and Blue Barred birds) you will know you are holding a pigeon who previously suffered from Rheumatic Fever which, in birds as well as in man, leaves the heart weakened. In such cases there are degrees of weakening mounting from very slight to very serious. If the 'white streak' is discovered hand the bird back to its owner with a polite request for an opportunity to inspect another specimen.

No, your inspection of the bird is by no means finished! It has hardly begun! Now pull down the bird's lower mandible (its lower beak) and squint into its mouth and throat. Across the throat, hanging down, is the serrated edged membrane we know as 'the curtain'. If you see that any part of it, or its whole, has been eaten away you will know that the bird has suffered from Canker. This is a very nasty pigeon disease caused by the Trichmonais germ. It is the same disease as Blackhead in Turkeys. I never keep a pigeon who is cankerous and I'm sure that you won't wish to import this fell disease into your loft. Canker is mainly hereditary as well as being highly infectious. If you find yourself holding a bird that has suffered from Canker listen to no tales about 'the bird has been cured' and so on. Just make your earliest possible polite excuse for vacating the premises.

While you have the bird's beak open, look up into the roof of the mouth and inspect the 'Slot'. This 'slot' (and it really looks like one) is at the rear end of the bird's nasal passage and every breath it takes in must pass through it. The edges of the slot must be quite clean and entirely without inflammation. Mucous in the slot, dried or not, or the inflammation of its edges, indicates that the bird is suffering from respiratory trouble. The presence of an off-white mucous in the mouth and/or throat is another symptom of this respiratory illness. If you find evidence of this kind politely inform the fancier that your time is up and you must be on your way.

Whenever you visit a loft (including your own) practise the art of standing perfectly still in it and letting your ears flap as they strain to detect that ominous snuffle, cough and rattle of the bird that is infected with respiratory ailment. If your ears and eyes detect the symptoms you need no other confirmation.

However, note the condition of the bird's wattle, the crinkly membrane that ornaments its nose. The wattle must be snowy white, unless the bird is feeding nestlings when the regurgitation of the food can stain the edge of the wattle. If the bird is not feeding youngsters but you detect staining of the wattle, what we call 'greasy-wattle', the bird is probably suffering from respiratory trouble. As above, now is the time for you to put a period to your visit.

Now pay attention to the bird's eye which Nature has fitted with three lids, the third one of which is called the Nictitating Membrane whose object is to keep the eyeball clean and polished. When this membrane flicks across the eye with the speed of a bullet the bird is fit and well. On the other hand, if you see this membrane fairly crawling across the eye with the speed of a tired snail you will know that the bird is sickening for something and that there is no point in you wasting more time on it.

While you are studying the eye, take out your magnifying glass and assess the value of its 'Eye-Sign' (as explained in another chapter of this book).

Hold the bird up before your eyes and study its head and neck. Does it appear to own a long neck when it is compared to the rest of its shape? If so, the bird has what we call 'a swanny neck' and, as you have already guessed, such types are far from being popular. Birds with 'swanny necks' also own long, spindly legs (instead of short, thick legs) and appear to walk on stilts. If the head is very flat on top (all hens are slightly flat on top but this feature must not be exaggerated) and the nose is over-dished, reject it. The beak must not be long and slender but short, thick and black (unless the bird has some white on its plumage when its beak will be light in colour, what we term 'soapy').

Always shy away from birds whose bodies give the impression of being wedge-shaped, viz. very wide across the chest but sharply tapering back towards the tail. What we are looking for, for want of a better description, is the 'boat-shaped' bird whose sides bulge with muscle (flesh) which when lightly pressed by the fingers resists the pressure like foam rubber. This Great Pectoral Muscle must not be hard, like hard rubber, especially at that place where it anchors to the bird's frame. When a pigeon becomes 'muscle-bound' after a long career of unremitting labour its pectoral muscle tends to deteriorate from the soft, spongy-like condition of well-toned young muscle to really hard flesh. This means that the muscle has lost much of its elasticity and is no longer an asset to the bird.

Birds acquired for the purpose of breeding should not be aged even though they had bred winners. An aged pigeon usually refuses to breed in a strange loft. This occurs even though the bird may have been fertile in its own loft. Some hens (the robust few) continue to lay eggs right up to their fourteenth year when Nature puts a period to their fertility. Always prefer young hens for producers. Old cocks often breed well when coupled to young hens but youngsters bred from really old hens usually look hag-ridden. Remember that young mothers breed the most robust off-spring.

Cocks of extreme vigour can breed up to around eighteen years of age but only the minority do. Longevity in pigeons has the same significance as in man. It means that the aged person, or bird, is extremely vigorous and of robust good health. The best long distance birds, and the breeders of such stock, will be bred from birds who retain their vitality and vigour into real old age.

Another point for the beginner to remember is that many pigeons start to grow internal tumours when they are six to seven years of age. Very few pigeons under six years of age grow tumours. Very few, indeed. In the majority of cases the tumour is of the 'benign' type which causes the bird no pain nor does it threaten its life. Unfortunately, in nearly all such cases, the tumour grows adjacent to the reproductive system and interferes with it, causing the hen to become barren and the cock sterile. This is yet another good reason for buying young stock. Tumours of the malignant type (the dreaded sarcoma) kill fairly quickly. It is not possible to diagnose the presence of a tumour inside a pigeon short of posting the bird and carrying out a post mortem.

While the bird is still in your hand 'span' the wing again and take special notice of the length of the two outside Primary flights (Numbers 9 and 10). Is the outside flight (the Number 10 'Pinion' flight) of the same length as its next door neighbour, the Number 9 Primary flight? If it is shorter than the Number 9 flight, is it shorter by more than ⅜ inch? If the answer is 'Yes' put the bird back on its perch and transfer your interest to another.

Your inspection of the bird is not yet at an end. Never accept any bird until you have given it the full inspection treatment. In any case, never part with any money until you have thoroughly investigated the bird's plumage. Naturally, a proper pigeon needs a thick coat of feather because it depends upon its plumage for the preservation of its life. What do you think would happen to a pigeon suddenly bereft of its feather in any but the warmest weather? The low temperature and its lack of bodily protection would so lower the bird's natural blood temperature that its urine would crystallise, a condition in which countless small crystals, each with needle sharp points and razor-sharp cutting edges, would appear. These crystals would soon pierce and rupture the skin of the kidneys so that the bird would soon be a total liability. Feathers grow on birds not for the purpose of enabling them to fly but to keep the body temperature high and the urine in its liquid form.

However, if you believe that the bird in your hand possesses adequate feather properties you may test the correctness of your assumption by trying to bare its keel. No feathers grow from the skin that is stretched across the keel-bone but feathers in adjoining tracts should overlap the keel so thickly that it is not possible for you to bare the skin over the keel with your fingers. Incidentally, if your fingers reveal the presence of a tiny little knob (like a small pimple) on the skin covering the keel, think nothing of it. Most pigeons grow this tiny knob in the same position.

Now test the feather for texture. Yes, feather texture is all important! The feather of the bird in your hand must be as smooth as silk. It must pass through your fingers with the high gloss of satin. Pigeon feather which is not of the texture of silk is the opposite, quite coarse. Silky textured feather is water-proof but this cannot be said for coarse feather. If the birds in the loft you are visiting for the purpose of acquiring stock are not convincingly of the silky textured type it is advisable for you to remember that you have another appointment to keep.

After handling a fit pigeon the front surface of your clothes will be liberally smothered with what appears to be white chalk. This powder from the bird's feather is what we call 'bloom'. It should lie thickly along the bird's back and on its feather. Where the Primary flights overlap, the uppermost feather's tip should leave its outline on the feather beneath it, etched in bloom. (Don't worry about the bloom on your clothing, it is easy to brush off.) When the bird shakes itself the air around it should be filled with a cloud of flying powder. Fit pigeons also leave 'bloom' as a film over water in which they have bathed. This 'bloom' is the product of the epidermis in the form of tiny flakes of skin and it is akin to the dandruff which falls from the moulting skins of people who have dry skin. It is a sure sign that the bird is enjoying a good moult and is therefore in an excellent state of good health.

Now, here is a very special hint indeed. If you pass your fingers under the wing butts of a sitting pigeon and the feather feels 'greasy' the bird must be at the peak of its physical fitness.

I think that by now I have given you plenty of hints on which to base your selection and if you apply them without fear or favour you should be able to select Foundation Stock with a measure of confidence. You must try and practice the art of selection because it will become one of your most responsible duties.

By the time you have rejected those pigeons whose external properties do not accord with the specification I have drawn up for you, you will know that the birds you have chosen, just because they are free of all the objectionable defects I have outlined, can have little that is wrong with them. Don't use my specification purely for the purpose of judging other fanciers' pigeons. Apply it with strictness to birds of your own breeding, ousting all those birds who betray even one of the above listed diversions from the true type.

In so many instances I have discovered that the successful fancier is one who constantly culls his stock, disposing without question or regret, of any bird who fails to meet the above specification and whose performance, as a racer or breeder, falls short of a high standard. Beginners who are reluctant or unwilling to subject their birds to strict testing, and speedily weed out the unworthy, have no future at all as pigeon fanciers.

One last word on this subject. Try hard to develop what we term 'an eye for a pigeon'. Examine each bird carefully and satisfy yourself that its physical parts are in balance. This term has no affinity with gravity. It means that the birds' body-parts must be in a state of symmetry. It must not be too long or too short, nor must it carry too much weight forward. A short tailed pigeon, such as one whose wing-tips reach the rear end of its tail, instead of ending some $\frac{3}{4}$ inch from the tail tip is abhorrent to me but I do not shy away from a bird whose tail is a mite longer than $\frac{3}{4}$ inch from the flight endings. These are what we term the 'long-casted' type of bird. One can see this feature in many champion long distance pigeons. An eye which is practised for seeing 'line' and 'balance' is an asset to the fancier.

The feather of a fit pigeon always stays 'tight'. This is to say that the surface of the plumage appears to be smooth and flat, like marble. When a pigeon 'blows' its feather (causing its feathers to lift and stand up instead of laying flat) it is usually ailing. In most instances of 'blown' feather the bird is feverish and running a temperature. Consequently, it opens up its feather to let the air get to its skin and cool it.

I imagine you are waiting for me to comment on the part that pedigree plays in the art of selecting stock? I always regard pedigrees as records of interest which make interesting reading. Some of them entertain me. However, the reader must remember that every racing pigeon that is hatched owns a pedigree, including the abnormal type, the deformed and diseased birds, the non-racing and non-homing kinds. They all have family trees whose names and numbers can be written down in the form of a pedigree. In my time I've collected countless pedigrees including some that cost a great deal of money. In the long term, not one of them was the slightest use to me.

The important truth is not that which is established when you discover that the bird's great-grandsire won a good position in a national race. Naturally, it is nice to know that the bird descends from one who put up a noble performance. The important truth (which few fanciers ever seem to discover) is in if the national

THE FOUNDATION STOCK

winner had any brothers or sisters, sons or daughters, who also covered themselves with glory? The real truth that you are seeking is whether the bird you propose to acquire came from an honest working family of birds, the type who work consistently and rewardingly, not in club races but in classic events. These include National, Combine, Specialist and Championship Clubs. Numbers and names written down on pieces of paper are meaningless in the form in which they are usually presented. Such things cannot be regarded as a substitute for consistently good work done on the road.

They say a good wine needs no bush. A good racing pigeon needs no pedigree – only a list of good performances of its own and its close relatives.

There is usually an error in the paper pedigree. Many of these errors are not known by the fancier who puts his pen to paper. For example, some cocks tread hens other than their own without the fancier knowing. Mistakes can occur when drafting pedigrees and some of these errors are not always purely accidental. In some instances they could be referred to as fortuitous. Never match two birds just because their paper pedigrees look good.

Whether you decide to found your loft on squeakers or adult pigeons, the information I have given you above should have taught you how to make a beginning which is shorn of the mistakes made by so many new starters who are ignorant of the technique of pigeon racing. Incidentally, don't be afaid of making a mistake because that is how we all learned to become pigeon fanciers.

If you take 24-day-old squeakers into your care you may have to feed them yourself for a while. Soak a supply of Tic Beans over night. Next morning tip away the water and pour warm water over the soaked beans. Do this just before you propose to feed the youngsters. You will have to pull down the squeaker's lower mandible (beak) and pop in the beans, one at a time, pushing them towards the bird's throat. After swallowing a few beans the youngster will cotton on to what is happening to it and it will help you out by holding its mouth open. Give each youngster fifty soaked beans at each feeding session which for a few days should be three times a day. Squeakers you feed yourself become the tamest birds in the loft, which reminds me that I never had a wild one who was also a big winner.

You teach a youngster to drink by immersing its beak (not its nose) in a small jar of warm water. It might back away the first time but eventually it gets thirsty and will drink.

I never knew a novice who was not attracted to large pigeons, or who did not despise small pigeons. In the old days many a new beginner called at my loft and tried to acquire pigeons from me. If I gathered the impression that the beginner was not too well breeched I would invite him to go into my young bird loft and help himself to a pair of squeakers. Incidentally, I went on impression, not on what I was told. In many instances the beginner would express his amazement when given a free hand to take what he liked. Well, I knew he would select the biggest squeakers in the misconception that they would necessarily be the best of the kit. One American new starter selected four pairs for himself and some weeks later he discovered he had selected seven cocks and one hen! I record the above more as a warning than as advice.

A nice, handy cock will have a total wing span (wing tip to wing tip) of some $27\frac{1}{2}$ inches. Don't accept this measurement as one that is final and binding. In pigeon racing we give a little either way. The finest long distance hen I ever handled in more than fifty years was a King's Cup Winner who had a single wing length of $8\frac{1}{2}$ inches when spanned. I like a cock to weigh about 16–17 ounces. A hen of the same quality would weigh an ounce or two lighter. I have known a champion cock to weigh 19 ounces but he was a rarity. Weight is a liability to everything that flies. Therefore, a heavily boned bird is at a disadvantage when compared with a more buoyant one.

The effect of breeding to line is to breed a better type. Why? Because some inbreeding of champion stock tends to bring about refinement of the type and part of the refining process is the slenderising of the bone. This means that the favoured long distance type of pigeon is usually of the medium or small-medium type. It gets its buoyancy from the lessening of the skeletal weight. For example, note the slender limbs of the racehorse when compared with the bone structure of the draught horse. Compare the bone structure of the whippet and greyhound with that of the more common breeds. Thus, in pigeon racing we prefer refinement of bone and line against the heavy and sometimes gawky over-weight pigeons.

The moral in all this is that you don't allow yourself to fall for the impressive big pigeons. Instead, you look around and find out what sort of bird is winning consistently in 'open' racing and buy accordingly. Remember that if you acquire big, heavy pigeons you will have to work them three times harder than the medium sized bird, in order to get them fit. At the same time, it is worth remembering that it will cost you three times as much to train the heavy ones, so such choice can be very expensive in the long run.

We have a saying in the sport which goes like this – 'Anyone can win pigeon races if he knows what to look for and how to find it.' No beginner should encounter much difficulty in this respect provided he studies this chapter well and commits it to his memory. Naturally, any intelligent fancier learns all that I have written down in fifty years of pigeon fancying, but who wants to labour on for half-a-century when it can all be learned in less than an hour?

V

The Art of Breeding

Our object as dedicated pigeon fanciers (and if you are not dedicated you will never become an Ace) is not just to keep and manage racing pigeons. The eternal hope that stimulates our undying loyalty to The Sport is that one day we shall breed a champion, even a great champion. It must be very thrilling to win a big race with a pigeon bred by someone else but even this exquisite, blood-tingling experience must pale beside the golden glory of breeding one's own classic winner! So, our real target as a fancier is to breed not just pigeons but winners, birds of the kind that are imbued with the winning streak.

'Old Hand' once wrote that there is no room in pigeon racing for the fancier with the dilettante approach. Instead, he called for nothing less than uncompromising dedication. After more than fifty years as a pigeon fancier I am able, with great certainty, to blame the few bad seasons I have experienced on my lack of concentration on my breeding problems during the off-season. Other issues, deemed to be more important at the time, were allowed to push the study of breeding projects into the back of my mind. I lived to regret my juggling with priorities when in a pigeon fancier's world there is only one. From October to March next year, in what we call 'the closed season', a fancier must let his mind constantly run over his proposed matings for next season, probing the possibilities of every proposed mating, weighing the imponderables, checking the conformities, always calculating what type of youngster any given coupling might produce.

Make up your mind from the moment that you start pigeon fancying that there is no future in just breeding pigeons. Anyone can do that who starts with one cock and one hen. Of what use to you is a loft stuffed with mediocre pigeons whose racing potential is nil? Pigeon corn is expensive and its price rises every year. When I was a boy pigeon corn cost twelve shillings per cwt and we thought that was expensive. By feeding good corn to non-working pigeons you only provide Rolls Royce motor cars for corn-raising farmers to own. If you approve the law of economics you will flatly refuse to feed even one pigeon who is unworthy of its perch. Let your ambition be perfectly simple and straightforward by assuring yourself that you will win the coveted King's Cup so that your memory becomes immortal. And to do that you must keep specially good pigeons of the very best type. What is even more important, you must learn how to breed pigeons of that calibre. The burning question now is 'how do I breed that kind of bird?'

I have studied this problem over many, many years. My experiments have probably cost many thousands of pounds to say nothing of the time I have contributed toward this end. And now, with what little hair I have left turned to a light shade of grey (worrying about pigeons has probably brought about this condition!) I have to admit that there is no hard-and-fast formula for breeding winners. If there is, I never discovered it. So there is no golden rule of this kind that can send us singing on our way. No amount of study given to Mendel's Law or to the Theory of Genetics can present us with the key to the mystery. There is one, and only one, way of bringing it off and that is by the process of subtraction. Perhaps another suitable synonym for the word 'subtraction' would be 'elimination'. In a pigeon sense it amounts to the same thing. In pigeon breeding we subtract birds, or eliminate them, in the process of forging ahead towards the production of our coveted champion long distance pigeon.

A remark of that kind needs explaining. In the chapter on Foundation Stock I described the kind of bird you should not buy. Similarly, the Ten Commandments tell you what you may not do. It all sounds very negative but, in fact, it is only by a process of elimination that we can hope to produce that elusive champion.

THE ART OF BREEDING

Be assured that no one can tell you what kind of a bird the future champion will be, only what he will not be.

After studying the specification drawn up by me in the chapter on Foundation Stock your mind's eye will mirror the kind of bird you don't want to breed and keep – the champion is the other kind.

It can be said of pigeons, as of men, that some are endowed with the mental qualities of the champion but lack the physique to stay the course. Of course, the reverse also applies, that we breed the kind of bird whose physique is adequate for a thousand mile race but who lacks the will to stick it out. Thus, our task as breeders of winners is three-fold, we must match the required mental qualities with those of physique and health.

Don't expect the matching of two champions of opposite sex automatically to produce more winners of the same calibre. They rarely do! Nature, whom we are told is the jealous creator of the species, is very critical of man's breeding intentions, especially when, like pigeon fanciers, he tries to overturn Nature's breeding policy. She has her own laws for governing the reproduction of a specie.

These natural laws, though immutable, are designed by Nature to preserve and perpetuate mediocrity. A great man once predicted that the meek would inherit the earth. Nature appears to desire the same end. Look around the lofts and what do you see? You see that for every good pigeon bred some twenty-four others are not going to make the grade.

I don't mean that the majority of the eggs laid will hatch out a mass of sub-standard and abnormal pigeons. We may be pleased, even dazzled, by the apparent physical beauty of our new season's crop but what happens when these young aristocrats are put along the road? Their numbers diminish at an alarming rate. The wastage rate is high! Every year in England alone well over a million pigeons fail to return to their home lofts and become strays. Why does this happen?

This climate is blamed for most of the losses. Look up back numbers of pigeon journals published in the autumn and winter and what do you read? That every succeeding Young Bird season is condemned as 'The Worst Ever'. In fifty and more years as a pigeon fancier I've never heard one Y.B. racing season referred to as 'good and satisfactory' but always the reverse. Most reports in the press end with the pious wish, that has never yet been granted, 'God grant that we never see another one like this!'

In spite of 'smash' seasons following each other with uncanny certainty it is impossible to meet a single fancier in the spring whose disposition could not be described as sunny. As his eye scans the occupants of his perches it does not see the ghosts of the birds who blew out last year, only potential champion after champion winking back at him. He is convinced that so far as he and his team are concerned the really nasty seasons with endless runs of bad luck have come to an end. The best is yet to come and it will come this new bright season that is about to open.

At the end of the 'bright, new old bird season' he will again be limping, crushed by the fantastic losses and the row of good hidings that left him with a record number of empty perches. His cup runneth over. But see, as August draws near and with it the opening of the Young Bird racing season his gloom disperses and his ship that was sunk is miraculously re-floated on 'The finest team of youngsters I ever raised!' No one could be in higher spirits as he transports his youngsters to the marking station.

Six weeks later the gloom re-descends. With his fine young bird team crippled, even almost non-existent, patched up with some hastily bred late-breds, his bruised mind bows to the approach of winter. He is not miserable for long. As the dark days pass so does he become more ebullient until the coming of the new breeding season finds him springy of step, with that typical, hopeful pigeon fancier's gleam twinkling in his eye. He knows, with a faith that shifts mountains, that the best is yet to come and that this will definitely be HIS YEAR. Like the rest of us he keeps coming back to lead once again with his jaw, merely for the pleasure he experiences in picking himself up to try again. It is of such stuff that the best of fanciers are made!

Nature hates and detests non-conformity. It necessarily follows that she also hates the production of winners because they do not conform to the mediocrity of the mass of losers. In any specie, a champion is necessarily an abnormal type, one out of the natural order. It has taken man many thousands of years to fashion the racing pigeon out of the original Rock Dove, converting the feral to the domesticated type, imbuing it with the extra power and energy needed to enable it to stay in the air for many hours on end. In Rome, nearly two thousand years ago, a writer named Ovid was complaining about the huge prices fanciers paid for racing pigeons and the hours they spent when talking about their birds. Ovid provides convincing evidence that man – and pigeon fanciers – haven't changed much over the ages.

The usual result of the mating of two champion racing pigeons is a number of mediocre pigeons. This dismal result has happened so many times, over so many years, that fanciers refer to the first generation of breeding from champions as 'The Fallow Generation'. So, Nature calls a halt in the production of those rare members of a specie that are brilliant, outstanding, exceptional to the mass of the rest.

The inevitability of 'The Fallow Generation' requires fanciers to be men of great patience. In my experience the new champion is most likely to be found in the g-children or g-g-grandchildren. There simply has to be a time lag in the generations of the family between the appearance of the exceptional 'greats'.

You are now invited to observe yet another facet (and a contradictory one, too) of Nature's policy of reproduction. She insists that even within the tight circle of an inbred family no two members shall be exactly alike! Thus, on the one hand she insists that a specie shall be populated by a conforming mass of mediocrity while, on the other, she insists on a measure of individuality. So, the great champion of Uniformity and mass mediocrity also brands every living member of a specie with the sign that makes him an individual who in some way or the other varies from his brothers and sisters, uncles and cousins. It is the combination of these two conflicting factors which makes pigeon breeding the complex and confusing issue it really is.

I know that when you first looked at a number of pigeons pecking around on a road, or a lawn, you were unable to distinguish one from the other, except possibly by noting a difference in plumage colours. To you, as to all laymen, racing pigeons are just pigeons. When you've seen one, you've seen the lot! I can remember hearing the white man say, 'All these coloureds look alike to me, can't tell one from the other,' and no doubt the coloured man says the same thing about the whites.

Once you become a fancier you start to study the birds and you soon discover that each one is recognisably different from the others, not only in appearance (in its phenotype) but also in character. In a matter of days under your observation each of your birds establishes its separate identity. You could recognise any one of them, anywhere. Before very long you are able to identify a pigeon in the air by the way it flies. This goes to prove what I have just written, that all pigeons are different.

While a study of Mendel's Law is unlikely to be of any direct benefit to you as a breeder his discoveries contain lessons that we, as fanciers, should take gratefully to heart.

Most school-leavers know that when Mendel crossed two unrelated families of the garden pea specie, mating a Tall variety with a Dwarf variety, he proved beyond question that one of the parents dominated the other through the progeny and, by the same token, that one of the parents submitted to such domination. In other words, Mendel found that one of the varieties was Dominant while the other was Recessive because in the first generation of the 'cross' all the progeny was Tall (not one dwarf). Yet, in the second generation of the cross the Dwarf variety reappeared to represent 25 per cent of the progeny (against 75 per cent Tall).

Thus, Mendel deduced from this result that the Tall variety was Dominant and he called the Dwarf variety Recessive because it lay hidden for a whole generation when it proved it was a pure strain, able to reappear in a following generation.

With the above in mind, I suggest that there are three aspects of Mendel's discovery which should interest pigeon breeders. Firstly, note that when Mendel crossed Tall with Dwarf he produced no medium-sized plants. Like its parents, the progeny was either Tall or Dwarf. Let this result convince you that it is useless for you to mate a large bird with a small one in the hope of breeding a medium-sized bird. The mating would produce only large and small pigeons, just like the parents.

Secondly, it would be an error for any fancier to assume (as so

THE ART OF BREEDING

many have already done) that when a male and female come together each contributes 50 per cent towards the creation of the new life. Students of genetics are taught that the chromosomic contribution of each parent is equal, viz. that each parent donates 50 per cent of the total number of chromosomes needed to create new life. This is correct but practical breeders (as opposed to those who deal only in theory) insist that the blood of one of the parents always dominates that of the other, exactly as Mendel discovered when he crossed his garden peas. Any fancier who proceeds to mate pigeons without this fact in mind is doomed to be bitterly disappointed.

Thirdly, did you ever ask yourself the question of whether Tall dominated Dwarf just because Tall is automatically Dominant while Dwarf is automatically doomed to be Recessive? It was the famous 'Old Hand' who first raised this problem and, in his inimicable way, set about supplying the answer. He said – 'No! Tall dominated Dwarf not because it happened to be Taller but because it happened to be the most vigorous of the two plants chosen by Mendel at the time he made his experiments.' He insists that Dwarf might well have dominated Tall had its growth been more vigorous than the Tall variety with which it was crossed. Size had nothing to do with it but vigour had. 'Old Hand' might well be correct, as is his habit when he is pontificating on a pigeon racing issue.

The abstract qualities of good racing pigeons include such virtues as 'The will to home,' 'The love of home,' 'Stamina,' 'Tenacity,' 'Vitality,' 'Virility,' and 'Vigour' with the latter A MUST. Realise then, that the dominant factor in all your matings must be Vigour with a capital V.

In pigeon racing we differentiate between an 'honest working pigeon' and one who is not reliable, who won't work properly and who is, therefore, patently dishonest. This divides racing pigeons into two categories, workers and non-workers, so that when you survey human society, and the animals of the fields and the forests, you realise, perhaps with a shock, that the two categories are universal.

This brings us to the definition of a good racing pigeon as being one who when tossed will home consistently and without any playing about on the way home. Hence the word 'consistent' and its eminence in the pigeon racing dictionary.

A pigeon who homes satisfactorily today, flying thirty miles in as many minutes, but who when tossed at the same spot tomorrow, in exactly the same weather conditions, returns in three hours instead of thirty minutes as on the previous day, cannot be considered to be a consistent pigeon. To the contrary, it is one on whom we keep our eye with a view to culling because this type of pigeon eats just as much corn as a consistent pigeon.

It is only by racing 'consistent' pigeons (a very small number in any loft) that we may find out at which distance each one is likely to excel.

The theory that claims that when two proven long distance pigeons are brought together more long distance birds will be produced is quite erroneous. The correct assumption is that they will breed long distance, middle distance, short distance and no distance birds. What is more, they will also produce strays and types too diverse to mention. Fanciers who look always for consistency in all things will be bound to conclude that the tools with which they are working must be considered to be very inconsistent. The fact is that there is no such thing as a gold-mine stock pair whose every nest contains a pair of youngsters stamped with the 24-carat sign. Anyone who thinks differently is not only destined to be disappointed, he will break his heart.

Before you have been a fancier very long you will hear others talking about the merits of Outcrossing, Inbreeding and Line-Breeding. Outcrossing means the mating of unrelated birds, Inbreeding the mating of relatives only and Line-Breeding means that the birds are bred to the male line with an occasional outcross (outcross=an unrelated bird). Note that as with human families, tribes, etc., the 'line' is through the father, son and g-son, who marry wives outside of their family group (usually unrelated, or slightly related). The family, as such, has only one line – the male – descending from the patriarch.

The only way to build a racing pigeon family is to learn how a family (or strain) is developed and then to practise it. My advice, which is founded on 'Old Hand's' precepts, would be 'Never bring in an unrelated male, only unrelated females.' The moment you bring in another cock for a cross you automatically break up the old family and start a new one. 'Old Hand' was 100 per cent right when he said that the quickest way to establish a strain of your own was to mate the Foundation Cock with his own daughters and raise a third or fourth generation before bringing in another unrelated hen.

No beginner should try and operate a system of close inbreeding. Only a very competent breeder could continually inbreed his pigeons and still stay in business. One has only to refer to the records of the past one hundred years of classic racing to discover that the majority of champions was the product of the first cross. One needs to own a good linebred family and to use 'a cross' (unrelated pigeon) in order to produce a champion.

Before putting two birds together it is necessary for you to study both of your selections when they are standing side by side. I recommend you to acquire a set of show pens (they are made of wire in sets of four) and place both the cock and hen in it. Now draw up a chair and sit down in front of the pens to study their characteristics.

Ask yourself if 'the balance' of one bird is complimentary to the other? The shape of the head, length of neck, the cast, colour of the iris, type of Eye-Sign, and so on. If both birds betray a certain boldness of the same factor you can count on their progeny stressing that factor to a greater extent.

Be particularly careful about the eye. I take for granted that you chose stock on the evidence of the Eye-Sign of the Producer type? Never mate two light-eyed birds together. Our object, always, is to deepen the iris colour, not to lighten it.

If you decide to found your loft on squeakers buy more than two pairs. I suggest a minimum purchase of ten pairs. Naturally, some club members will raise their hands in horror if you tell them you propose to train and race the youngsters you have purchased. They will probably press you to 'breed from them first and get your money's worth before you lose them'. That advice is all very well but if you don't work the youngsters how do you know they will be worth breeding from? Supposing the sellers sold you a load of rubbish? Isn't it better for you to discover this fact in a matter of months instead of waiting years to find out that you have been working with worthless pigeons? If you wait to test out the value of your birds as breeders they could eat their way through a ton of food before you saw the light!

The value of a pigeon can only be proved by its work on the road. By racing the youngsters you will be given at least one kind of satisfaction – that next season you will be breeding from birds you have proved beyond doubt are willing to work.

There is a vast difference between a hard-worked piegon and one who is over-worked. The problem is in knowing when hard-work has been exceeded. All racing pigeons should be hard-worked but none should be over-worked. Young pigeons should be kept working all the time, never missing a day except for bad weather. Pigeon racing is not the sort of game that lends itself to any consideration but the most demanding. Don't treat your pigeons as birds who need to be pampered and cossetted. Pigeons, like racehorses and greyhounds, are not pets but athletic animals who are required to work for their board and lodging.

If you entertain any doubts about a pigeon's health it must go. Allow one sick bird to stay in a loft and in no time at all others will go down and the 'form' will disappear. The aim must be to breed better pigeons from the best you have in the loft. Racing pigeons are steadily improving, generation by generation, in the hands of the intelligent minority who far from being easy to please constantly demand an improved type of pigeon. Fanciers like myself, who flew birds over fifty years ago, are in a position to compare modern birds with the ancient and decide whether the strains have improved. The truth is that the modern bird is very much better than its ancestors of fifty years ago.

How much better? The modern bird is no longer fed an all-grain diet. Under the enlightened management of the modern fancier racing pigeons are given a scientifically compounded diet which is enriched by a proper balance between vitamins and minerals. This means that it matures more quickly and attains a higher degree of fitness. Because it is fitter it tends to fly longer at exercise. Properly fed and managed youngsters will never fly less than one hour per day but will stay up for the best part of two hours. This urge for more prolonged exercise swells the muscles and produces a larger, athletic heart. Therefore, from the hatching to the age of maturity the bird is more robust and better able to indulge its biological promptings. The common assaults on the health of young birds, including anaemia, are now stood off and no longer set back the maturing infant. The new and better dietry enables the fancier to bring his birds into 'racing form' much more quickly than of yore.

In the long ago only once did the British Fancy essay a 1,000-mile race. This was in 1913, from Rome, and only two birds ever returned. One of these, Hudson's 'King of Rome,' took a month to negotiate the course. In 1945 my 'Per Ardua', a six-month-old hen, flew Gibraltar to England, 1,098 miles, in 14 days. All of that was in the past. Today racing pigeons are flying 1,000 miles every year and it won't be long before we reach out for 1,500 miles. What kind of limits can one impose on wonder pigeons?

The beginner's greatest frustrations will overtake him when he is looking round for a probable Producer Hen. The truth is that there are not enough good producer hens to go round so that most fanciers fail to get their fair share of the available supply.

The ratio of good cocks to hens is about ten to one (some fanciers think my odds should be lengthened). This state of affairs stems directly from fanciers' failure to raise enough good hens. It is a fact that the chance of any hen surviving both the nest and the training pannier is chronically much smaller than the life expectancy of the male. The baby hen is more delicate than the cock and always comes off second best when the nest pair stretch up their beaks for food. It astonishes me that so many fanciers seem to be unaware of the disadvantages suffered by the baby female in the nest. They are never given an even break. I breed my producer hens by single-rearing them, thus overcoming the blatant inequality of the nestbowl.

Single rearing baby hens is not the complete answer to the problem. The frailties of the hen will again be made manifest when the youngsters are trained. In most seasons it will be found that the loss of young hens is greater by far than the loss of young cocks. Note that the cock does not have to support the burden of a reproductory process and the ills that go with it. The most remarkable thing about hens is that in long distance racing the hen usually has the 'edge' on the cocks. Whereas a goodly number of cocks can be rated as 'Medium-good', hens tend to be 'Medium-exceptional' or 'Medium-Useless'. A classification of this kind is inevitable when the sex-ratio in the Performance Stakes is ten to one.

The genetic structure of cocks and hens must also be taken into consideration. Among the billions of genes which make up the 'blue-print' of the specie there is one which carries many of the factors that are of prime importance to your future plans. It is known as 'The Sex-gene' and its influence on the breeding is immense. It is known that both sire and dam pass their sex-genes to their sons but only the cock can pass his sex-gene to his daughters, the hen cannot. It is this 'sex-gene factor' which accounts for 'Sex-Linkage', as with colour inheritance.

When describing the difference between Inbreeding and Line-Breeding I stressed the importance of breeding to the male line. Perhaps you wondered why I did not suggest breeding to the female line? Well, because the hen can't pass her sex-genes to her daughter the female line does not and cannot exist as a practical proposition. In any case, those who have tried to breed a 'female line' have always lived to regret it. The cocks tend to become henny looking and are under-sized. Eventually, difficulty is encountered in breeding cocks.

It has been known for many years that whereas the 'first cross' on a line-bred family can produce a champion the second and third generations of the cross can be very fallow indeed. This is because the 'vigour' of the first cross tends to fade in the second and third generation, evaporating, so to speak. This can be seen if we refer back to my third reference to Mendel's discoveries above. Note that in the first cross of Tall with Dwarf the first generation progeny were all Talls. Not one dwarf was reproduced. But, when the same All Tall plants were again self-fertilised the next generation contained 75 per cent Tall and 25 per cent Dwarf. Why? Because the vigour of the first generation cross had declined by as much as 25 per cent in one generation of breeding thus giving us positive proof that vigour decreases when inbreeding is indulged in. If that is so, and you must admit the result is more than likely, why inbreed at all? The answer, albeit reluctant, is that one must preserve the type and all its good characteristics

THE ART OF BREEDING

and there is only one way of doing this, viz. by good line-breeding methods. The above explains to you why a 'cross' is absolutely necessary. However, after bringing in the 'cross' make haste to breed it out by mating all its progeny back to the 'old blood' of the family.

At this stage we may pause to summarise what we think we have learned up to now about the art of breeding. Firstly, we must go all out to buy, beg, or borrow really outstanding producer hens. Secondly, we must never use an unrelated cock for a 'cross'. We breed only from our own cocks who in every instance will be the lineal descendant of our one Stud Sire.

It is very easy to recognise a good Producer Hen. She will breed winners with any good cock. I wish I could say the same about every Producer cock.

So much for the Theory of the Art of Breeding. Now for some practical hints.

You have made up your mind about your first mating. Remember, however, that up until now the cock and hen you propose to bring together were previously mated to another bird so what you are proposing to do is to break up two old matings and bring about a new one. If your nestboxes are of the 'Swinging Door' design described in this book you have only to place the hen in one side and close the door, thus locking her in, while you place the cock in the other side, also locking him in the box. They can now regard each other through the dowelled partition. If you own no divided nestboxes you are advised to knock up a mating-up box on the lines of the Swinging Door nestbox.

Now note the behaviour of the two birds. It is possible that the cock, or the hen, even both, may want to sit and sulk. What we are waiting to see is the cock make a sexual display towards the hen (sweeping his fanned tail along the floor, inflating his interclavicular air sac and coo-ing loudly) and the hen respond by partly fanning her tail and nodding her head towards the cock. Both birds must stay penned away from each other until they start to caress through the bars of the partition. Then, and only then, is it safe for them to be allowed together. The sulking can, in extreme cases, last for up to four or five days. I've never known either a cock or hen of breeding age fail to mate in that time, always providing that their old partners were not living in the same loft and within seeing or hearing range.

It is preferable for you to acquire odd pigeons, not pairs. My advice is never to buy a mated pair which, more often than not, will probably refuse to breed in a strange loft. I can remember loaning a pair of blue chequers to an experienced fancier friend who lived some 100-miles away. He kept the birds some six weeks but failed to persuade them to breed in his loft. His letter said, 'they sit beside each other but the cock never caresses the hen, he neither drives nor treads. As for the hen, she sits on her perch all day long and looks bored.' In desperation he returned them to my loft and as they flew from his hand to the floor the cock trod the hen.

Racing pigeons are not machines, nor are they always predictable. They are as different as human beings are different and, in the main, just as intractable. So don't expect all of your birds to behave in the same way, to respond in the same way, and to work in the same way.

Never, never let a cock scalp a hen, a fate she may suffer if put into a box with a strange cock and take care to protect the squeakers from being scalped. This occurs in many lofts because proper precautions have not been taken by the fancier.

Once mated a pair of pigeons will stay mated until one or the other dies, fails to return to the loft from a training or race toss, or until the owner forcibly breaks up the mating. A racing pigeon will look around for a new mate if its mate fails to put in an appearance in a day or two.

The nestbox belongs to the cock, not to the hen. It is inadvisable for you to take the cock away from his nestbox and try and get him to settle in another. He may take the new nestbox but he will still try and fight the cock who takes over his old nestbox. When you change a mating the hen must be taken to the cock, not vice versa.

If you wish all the eggs laid by your mated pairs to be fertile you must ensure that only one pair of birds at a time is let out of the nestboxes to eat and drink, etc. My practice is to let out one pair every hour to enjoy the liberty of the compartment. In this way, in an eightbox loft compartment each pair enjoys one hour of liberty per day. I keep this schedule running until the hens have

THE ART OF BREEDING 73

laid both eggs and then all the birds are given the liberty of the compartment. A system of this kind ensures a high hatchability rate and guarantees the parentage of the squeakers. If all birds are free in the compartment the cocks will stop another from treading his hen and the result may be clear eggs. At the same time, the wrong cocks may be treading the hens.

The average time taken by a hen to lay her eggs is eight days from time of mating, always provided the cock is chasing and treading the hen. A number of factors can interfere with this egg-laying period, including extra cold weather, the age of the hen, attacks by parasites, etc.

Never mate last year's late-breds (birds hatched after the last day in June) until late April or May of the following year. Never expect a maiden hen to be a reliable sitter.

Another question that arises is that of fertility. Beginners are puzzled when one egg of a nest pair hatches but the other does not. This happened because the hen was allowed to stand over her first egg. This prevented the cock from chasing and treading her to fertilise her second egg. I advise you to take away the first egg directly it is laid and to return it only after she has laid her second egg. The alternative is to shut the hen out of the nestbox for the whole of the day following the laying of the first egg. The hen cannot lay fertile eggs unless the cock is continually chasing her and giving her slight pecks on the head, with periodical treading. The chasing is, of course, punctuated by tender nestbox caressing.

The hen will lay her first egg about five o'clock in the afternoon. Her second egg should arrive about two o'clock on the afternoon of the day following the day after laying the first egg. Once laid, both birds will sit the eggs in turn, the hen taking the night stint. Some eighteen-and-a-half days later the eggs should hatch. This period of incubation can also vary slightly according to the weather.

Take a good look at the eggs before allowing the birds to incubate them. Is the shape of the egg perfect, pointed at one end and blunt at the other? Is the texture of the shell beautiful to behold, with no bumps and ridges, no disfigurements? Is the shell exceptionally smooth, silky, milk-white, almost approaching the colour of Mother O' Pearl? If you can't answer with a ready and unqualified 'yes' to the above questions toss the eggs into the dustbin and let the birds go to nest again. If a hen persists in laying faulty eggs get rid of her. A faulty egg hatches out a faulty youngster.

When the eggs have incubated for ten days take them up and hold them between your eye and a strong light source. Has the egg darkened and lost its new laid opaqueness? Does it appear to contain a dark mass? If so, the egg is fertile because the embryo inside it is developing. If not, the egg is infertile and should be thrown away. It is not sensible for one to permit a hen and her mate to go on sitting an extra nine days on unhatchable eggs.

If you visit your loft one morning and find that several nests contain stone cold eggs which have apparently been deserted by the sitting birds you can be quite sure they were frightened off the nests. The commonest reason for deserted eggs is attack by Red Mite. A sitting bird will stand up to a rat but it cannot withstand an attack by an army of Red Mite. The fancier must use the necessary specifics for warning off Red Mite and other parasites. At the same time, ensure that animals (rats, stoats, cats, dogs, foxes, squirrels, etc.) cannot get into the loft.

Nestlings require no food on the day they hatch. They live on the remainder of the yolk which they absorb into their bodies during the hatching. From then, onwards, for four to five days, the parents will feed them with the special 'milk' or curd which they manufacture on their breasts. This curd begins to grow on the breast of both sitting cock and hen after they have been incubating the eggs for some eleven to twelve days. Fanciers often refer to this 'curd' as 'pigeon-milk' or 'soft-food'. The curd is very, very rich in nutrients (the protein content is about 32 per cent). The best foster-parents are those who can make this curd last longer than 4/5 days. At the expiry of the curd-making period (4/5 days) the parent birds begin to feed their nestlings on soaked grain through the process of regurgitation.

When the squabs hatch they are covered with yellow, downy hair. Really healthy specimens are endowed with a huge mane of down hair which can be seen as it protrudes through the plumage for some weeks after the youngster has become fully feathered.

THE ART OF BREEDING

Where the youngster's down is short (short-downed) it is showing the typical characteristic of the Recessive.

Well fed nestlings grow very fast indeed. They double their weight in their first 48 hours of life. When you study them in their nests their crops should appear to be bigger than their whole body and be well packed with food at all times. It is a fact that a nestling eats its own weight in food per day. Any squeakers who go short of food when in the nest will not develop into robust old birds. Birds of all kinds are enormous eaters when compared with human beings, size for size. Some adult pigeons eat their own weight in food in a week.

By the 6th/7th day feathers will begin to shoot and continue to develop until the 25th day. It is at this stage that squeakers reach their maximum weight. The last feathers to develop are those under the wing. Feathers do not grow on every part of the skin, only in tracts but they manage to cover up the areas of skin which do not grow feathers.

At the 5th to 7th day after hatching the beginner must remember to slip a Union metal registration ring over the claw of one leg because after one week from hatching the bird's claw will reach maximum size and be too big to pass through the aperture of the metal ring. Nestlings whose parents are given 'boost' diet may well reach maximum claw size in some 4/5 days so will need 'ringing' earlier. Watch the thickness of the developing leg.

When the youngsters are fourteen-days old the cock will start to 'look at his hen again' and she should lay another round of eggs when her nestlings by the previous round are three weeks old. In most cases the hen will stop feeding her youngsters when she lays her next round of eggs but the cock will continue to feed them until they are weaned (taken away from their parents and taught to eat and drink for themselves). If weaned, babies should be taken away at about 24 days of age.

I have described the nest routine, which is simple enough. Pigeons are quite capable or rearing their youngsters without our assistance. All they require is good, balanced diets, and plenty of good food and very, very clean drinking water.

Please look out for any undesirable features and in the early days of hatching take a bucket of water into the loft when you do your rounds of the nests.

If you find a nest where the youngsters' droppings are wet, loose and messy bucket them at once. The youngsters are constitutionally weak and will never make up into robust old birds. In some instances the cause of the wet, messy droppings can be traced to one or more of the parents being what we term 'wet feeders'. This means that instead of packing the youngsters' crops with food the parents have pumped water into them. In a case of this kind dispose of the nestlings and the parent(s) responsible.

Nestlings who can't sit in the nestbowl and hold their heads up should also be bucketed. When the nestlings are five days old, wait for the sitting parent to leave the nest and then place the palm of your warm hand down over the back of each nestling in turn. Grip the baby firmly but gently and turn it over. If you find its navel is blue bucket it immediately. At the same time, take a look at its keel-bone. Is it straight and true?

If you hear a youngster keeping up a continuous piping noise (not the squeaks made by all babies at feeding time) bucket it. What I am trying to tell you is the art of culling as practised by experienced fanciers and how to keep it up from the time the egg is laid and onwards. This eternal culling must never be abandoned. It must be pursued at every stage.

Try poking your fingers at the nestlings. They should rock back on their legs while the male in the nest should peck at you. Now, if both of them stand up on their legs, instead of rocking back, they, too, should finish up in the bucket. A nestling with a packed and contented crop would not be strong enough to stand up under the weight, hence it rocks back. If they can stand up on their legs they are obviously not receiving enough food to nourish their growth and make them robust. Here again, suspect the value of the parents as stock birds. Never keep squeakers with small crops.

Tolerate no visible sign of weakness in a squeaker. I know it is very difficult to be ruthless with pigeons but you must make up your mind from the very outset whether you wish to keep pigeons as pets, or as racers. If you wish to race and win, sentiment, or any similar emotion, must be suppressed. Your golden rule must be

THE ART OF BREEDING

that only the fittest will be allowed to survive. Try and preserve the lives of weaklings and your future is nil.

If you don't cull from the nests you will be lumbering yourself with weaklings who will later go down when worked. Tragic setbacks and heartbreaks are reserved for those fanciers who shrink from perpetual culling.

Don't say to yourself 'that squeaker is valuable because it is off so-and-so' or because it was bred from birds who cost the earth to buy. Go purely and simply on the bird's physical conditions on the day it hatches and onwards. Never forgive a nestling who does not develop naturally. When in doubt, dispose.

Squeakers always display a natural reluctance to feed themselves. Do your best to interest them in the routine of self-help by placing pots of food and water in the nestboxes. When they see their parents eating and drinking they will be tempted to emulate them.

In lofts where it is intended to wean youngsters at 24 days of age it will be found that when taken away from their parents they will refuse to eat and drink, that is, if they were not able to learn how to do so before being weaned. The responsibility now devolves upon you. Teach them to drink by holding them with beak (not nose) immersed in water. They may refuse at first time of asking but after a few tries they will start to drink like a horse (sucking up the water).

If a youngster goes for two days without a meal it will develop a fret-mark on the quill of the primary it is growing. The fret-mark is in the form of a crease or dent across the quill. Or it might develop wishy-washy lines across the plumage and tail rectrices. If you wean your youngsters before they can fend for themselves you will have to feed them yourself, three times a day, with soaked beans, probably for upwards of a week.

A missed meal is always a tragedy for a bird. To be subjected to an erratic or sub-standard diet when it is young is to prevent the bird from ever maturing as a useful racer or breeder. They say that pigeon fancying can be as hard as you make it but this is just another of those pigeon 'sayings' which is not strictly true. Pigeon keeping and racing is a 365-days-a-year job. Further, the fancier must spend as many hours a day as possible in his loft.

If the birds are fed on mixed grain they need 2 ounces per bird per day, more if feeding youngsters, in fact, robust youngsters are the result of parents having a permanent access to food (by way of hopper, etc.). If fed on beans only, the birds need 1 ounce per day but they would also need a supplementary 'boost' to go with the beans. I recommend every beginner to install a hopper for feeding old birds.

Before squeakers become wing-strong (able to fly up onto a perch) take them outside the loft and stand about 3/4 feet from the edge of the open Trapping Corridor. Take each squeaker in turn and let it flutter from your hands into the corridor and land on the wooden (or preferably tiled) floor. Do this every day until the bird is wing strong. At the same time, gradually extend the distance between your hands and the trapping corridor.

You busy yourself with this process because you are teaching your babies how to fly in through the 'Open Door'. In short, you are investing in the future by making sure that on race day you will be able to 'make a fast catch' and thereby save precious seconds. The seconds saved by the fast catch make all the difference to a pigeon's race velocity, often as much as is needed to record a winning instead of a losing time. Thus, the youngsters are taught to fly out of the air and in through the 'open door.'

Now is the time to impress on your birds that you are well aware of the power of the incentive. Before letting your first squeaker go, to fly in, sprinkle the corridor floor with mixed oil seeds. A fifty-fifty mixture of hemp and linseed should provide the necessary incentive. Pigeons love hempseed and rave over it. They are not so keen on the linseed (which is very, very good for them) but with the taste of the hemp on their tongues they will take up some of it.

At this stage of writing this book I pause to make an observation. It is that fanciers who allow themselves to be persuaded to write textbooks for pigeon fanciers (and a great deal of persuasion was used by my colleagues before they induced me to put this lot down on paper) do so under the impression that they are not only trying to add a little more to our sum of knowledge of the sport but that here and there a reader who is not reading us for sheer entertainment may take our words to heart and begin to practice what we are preaching.

We entertain these thoughts not merely because they are sweet (who wouldn't like to have a protégé?) but because we are driven by a genuine desire to smooth and ease the road the beginner must travel if he pines for advancement.

Every sport, no matter what its nature, is based on technique which, in its widest sense, means skilled practice that is subject to discipline. The object of this textbook and any other written for pigeon fanciers is to describe and explain a technique without which no lasting success is possible.

There are no bad techniques for the simple reason that technique is founded only on accomplishment so that any beginner who studies a textbook and puts its teaching into effect is certainly going to reach his goal faster and with more confidence than the new starter who launches himself on a sea of ignorance.

Some people are lucky enough to be born with real talent and flair but no amount of inborn trait can achieve success until it has been disciplined by the proper technique, therefore, the intelligent beginner must set about the task of learning how to practice as a pigeon fancier who follows the correct technique. Some try to pick up technique from local fanciers, learning a bit here and a bit there. The quick road to the top is still through the pages of a textbook and the student who makes such a book his preceptor wastes no time on his way.

Don't forget what you've read the moment you close the book and put it down. Go over, and over, and over one passage, committing it to memory, before you turn to the next. No one could absorb the information given in this book in one reading session, or merely by reading it through once. I suggest that the relative chapter is read through several times at the appropriate time of the year viz. chapter on Breeding late February, early March, on Training in April and July, and so on, by way of a refresher course. Discipline yourself, as well as your birds, to do certain things (such as studying) at certain set times as a kind of routine which is never changed or dropped. That is the way to become an Ace.

VI

The Plumage Colours

The true glory of a racing pigeon is to be found in its racing performances but its physical glory is undoubtedly in its plumage colour, the texture of its feather and, fourthly, in its eye. However, the colour of the plumage is of less importance than its feather texture. There is no case for suggesting that colour has any influence on the bird's performance. Colour preference is just a matter of the fancier's choice.

I have no room in this book for dealing with the whole range of plumage colours and shades that make up the pigeon world. One could write a book on this subject alone. I shall refer only to the common plumage colours that can be found in most pigeon lofts.

In a previous chapter I referred to 'sex-linkage'. This mention arose out of the hen's inability to pass her sex-gene to her daughters. This genetic factor was first noticed by poultry breeders who found that when a Rhode Island Red cockerel was mated to a White Sussex hen the progeny consisted of All White Cocks and all Red hens. Note the criss-cross inheritance of the sons taking the plumage colour of their dams and the daughters the colour of their sires.

A further example in pigeon breeding is shown when we pair a Blue Chequer Cock to a Red Chequer Hen, the progeny will consist of Red and Mealy Cocks and Blue Chequer and Blue Barred Hens.

Colour is subject to the principles of Mendelian Law (see chapter on 'The Art of Breeding') which is why some colours are Dominant and others Recessive. A colour is Dominant when all the progeny are of its colour and not that of the matched mate. For example, if an Ash Red cock is mated to a Blue Barred hen all the progeny will be red coloured because Ash Red is the Dominant Red colour.

Scientists discovered only four basic and true colours in pigeon plumage. They are Black, Blue, Brown and Red. Because white plumage contains no pigment it is no colour at all. The four Intense Colours are (as mentioned above) all Dominant and all other colours are 'Recessive' and known as 'dilutes' of the Intense colours. Obviously, if a pigeon with Dominant plumage colour is mated to one with 'dilute' colour the Dominant colour will dominate the plumage of the progeny.

The dilute of Black is Dun (a yellowish shade), while Silver is the dilute of Blue. Silver is actually silver-grey in colour. The dilute of Brown is Drab and Yellow is the dilute of Red.

Controversy exists on the subject of Blue. Is it, or is it not, a Dominant colour? Some fanciers insist that Blue is the dilute of Black and quote the result of mating Dominant Black with Blue (all offspring will be Black) as their criterion. However, if a loft of pigeons was left to self-mate and no cross was brought in for many generations all the plumage colours would be Blue Barred, as in the original Rock Dove. It should also be noticed that in a mating of male and female Blue Barred, all the progeny are Blue Barred!

Equally controversial is the subject of Red plumage. No one seems to be sure of how many different Reds are to be found. In fact, it appears that there are four types, only one of which is Dominant. All Dominant Reds have their wing tips plum coloured, or 'ash' coloured, hence the title 'Ash Red'. No black tics or splashes will be found on Dominant (Ash) Red plumage. These dark markings are found only on the feather of Recessive Red feathers. Even then, the markings are restricted to the cocks.

Brown plumage is referred to as 'Chocolate' and it is extremely rare in Great Britain.

The Recessive nature of Silver is stressed when it is produced from a mating of Blues. It is always a hen! Those fanciers who like to breed Silvers and wish to produce Silver Cocks, as well as

Silver hens, must first mate a Blue Barred Cock to a Silver Hen. Both the progeny will be Blue Barreds. The Blue Barred Cock from this mating must then be mated to its Dam (the Silver Hen) to produce Silvers and Blues of both sexes. Personally, I do not recommend beginners to cultivate dilute colours.

Grizzle is a rare colour, probably because it appeals to only a few fanciers. It is also a Dominant one. Therefore, a Grizzle mated to a Blue produces all Grizzles but if two Grizzles are mated together they will produce Grizzles and some Blues.

Blue Barred Cock to Blue Cheq Hen can breed Blue and Blue Cheq Cocks and Blue and Blue Cheq Hens (no Reds or Mealies). Mealy Cock with Blue Barred Hen breeds Mealy Cocks and Hens and Blue Cocks and Hens. Note the sex-linkage when Red Cheq Cock is mated to Mealy Hen. Red Cheq Cocks and Hens, Mealy Cocks and Hens, Blue Cheq and Blue Hens.

The basic colour of a pigeon's plumage, as instanced in the Rock Dove, from whom all our birds are descended, is Blue. The Blue carries two Black Bars across its wings and a further black bar across the end of its tail feathers. A Blue Cheq also has two black bars on its wing but, in addition, it has 'Chequer' marks on its wings. These cheq marks really represent a third bar which has broken up and spread over the wing.

A Black Cheq differs from a Blue Cheq in the feature of its chequering which is denser and without the blue background. Black Velvet is an all Black wing in which the chequering has given way to a solid black.

The silkiest of feather is found on the Red Chequer. I cannot recollect ever handling a Red Chequer whose feather was in any way coarse but I have noticed this condition in Blue and Black Cheq. This indicates that it is wise to use Reds in the breeding.

A plumage colour can be 'hardened' when it is mated with an opposite Intense colour. For example, to increase the depth of Red mate with solid Black. If opposites are not used the plumage colours tend to lighten and to a certain extent lose solidity.

Avoid birds whose plumage colour is wishy-washy. Ensure that the wing chequering is always clearly defined and not blurred round the edges. The Black Bars on the wing should also be solid, well defined, clear cut against the blue background.

What we term Smokey Blue is also a Dominant Intense colour. The white on rump and outside tail feathers disappears, while the markings on the wing coverts are blurred and the blue areas are darkened.

A lot more work must be done on white before we are able to say that it is Dominant or Recessive although its Recessive nature occurs in Pieds, a name we give to the plumage of a racing pigeon when it contains white on the coverts, or on the head, breast, etc., or a tick at the corner of the eye. Where a pigeon has one or more flights in the wing it is referred to as being 'White-Flighted'. When the white areas of the plumage are approximately equal to 50 per cent of the bird's plumage, the bird is referred to as being Gay Pied. Pied markings are recessive and can appear after a number of generations of no Pieds.

VII

The Diet

When I was a beginner in the year 1919 fanciers used to say to me, 'He who masters the secret of feeding racing pigeons has learnt how to win out of turn.' This is not strictly true and it only fits where it touches, so to speak. Obviously, no athlete is going to excel if it isn't fed properly, but what constitutes 'proper feeding' in this day and age?

What no beginner should do is rush down the road to his local Corn Chandler and stock up with grain on the assumption that if he feeds his birds on the best corn that money can buy they will naturally respond by winning races. Instead, let us sit down and quietly get to grips with what really constitutes a proper pigeon diet in the light of what we know about food nutrients today as against what none of us knew fifty years ago.

The racing pigeon is, of course, a granivorous type, which is to say that in the wild state it eats grains and seeds, not meat. And therein lies the specie's greatest weakness, as I shall try and explain in this chapter.

I shall begin by saying that what was good enough for the origin of our birds, the Rock Dove, is not good enough for the modern racing pigeon for the simple reason that whereas the Rock Dove only made limited daily scouting flights in search of food the modern racing pigeon is often called upon to undertake more work in a day than the Rock Dove flew in months. The strain and drain on the modern racing pigeon's store of energy and body tissues is enormous compared with the work output of the Rock Dove, such as flying a thousand miles in several days and upwards of 600/700 miles on a single day! The racing Pigeon's diet must enable the bird to store up vast surpluses of energy and also – and this is very, very important – restore body tissue quickly and effectively.

Grain is grown from cultivated grasses, so it necessarily follows that it will have inherited all the vices as well as the virtues of this ancient form of food. What are these vices? In the first place, grain contains no Silicon yet with the exception of the down feather every pen on a pigeon's body calls out for this vital chemical. A shortage of Silicon can weaken the tensile strength of feather quill and there is no silicon in grass. It is for this reason that grass stalks bend and break so easily. Another of the shortages in grain concerns vitamins and minerals.

Apart from its obvious and serious shortages grain contains too much carbohydrate and not enough protein which is the tissue-building nutrient.

Those fanciers who have studied dietry and learnt the part played by both vitamins and minerals in food, know that an all-grain diet cannot in itself supply the bird with all it needs by way of nutrients, yet the majority of fanciers still try and maintain their birds on a diet which probably originated with Noah. Modern scientific research and its results leave us in no doubt that it is apparent that grain diets must be supplemented by additional nutrients, vitamins and minerals, if the bird is to develop the kind of robust good health which is consistent with 'racing form'. In other words, we now live in the age of enriched dietry, for human beings and for animals.

The grains commonly used in pigeon diets can be divided into three categories: (1) The Legumes, which include Beans, Peas and Vetches (Tares); (2) the Cereals, which include Wheat, Maize, Barley, Oats, Rice and Dari; (3) The Oil Seeds which include Hemp, Linseed and Rape.

The highest protein content is found in the Legumes. Beans 25 per cent, Peas 22 per cent and Vetch 26.1 per cent. The Cereals are not so rich in proteins. Maize (Indian Corn) 10 per cent, Wheat 12 per cent, Barley 9 per cent, Dari 10 per cent, Rice

THE DIET 87

6.8 per cent, Oats 10.3 per cent. The Oil Seeds contain Hemp 18 per cent, Linseed 24 per cent, Rape 19.5 per cent.

The minimum protein requirement of a racing pigeon is 16 per cent. Many, many experiments on pigeons prove that diets with a protein content of less than 16 per cent lead to deterioration in the bird's health and to emaciation of its body. If we take 16 per cent of protein as our guide it becomes obvious that a diet of cereal grains only is a starvation diet. People who have seen street pigeons living on scraps of bread and biscuit have been foolish enough to claim that pigeons don't need a high-protein diet. They are foolish because not one of those roadsters could fly 500-miles on the day, or breed robust progeny that could fly the clock round. Bear in mind that the yolk of a pigeon's egg contains 32 per cent of protein, the minimum required to feed a new life.

However, those who formulate pigeon diets are not only concerned with their protein content because there are other important dietry factors needing attention. In all food there must be a percentage of carbohydrate (the chief constituent of cereal grains) which, unlike protein, is not there to stimulate growth but to provide the body with some heat and energy. Unfortunately, it is the carbohydrate content of food that also provides the athlete's worst enemy, fat! The carbohydrate content of the grains is as follows :

LEGUMES

Tic Beans – 49.9 per cent; Peas – 56 per cent; Vetch (Tares) – 50.7 per cent.

CEREALS

Maize – 69.2 per cent; Wheat – 69.2 per cent; Barley – 67.6 per cent; Dari – 67.9 per cent; Rice – 78 per cent; Oats – 58.1 per cent.

OIL SEEDS

Hemp – 21 per cent; Linseed – 22.9 per cent; Rape – 18 per cent.

On the face of it, the Carbohydrate percentages quoted above appear to indicate that the Oil Seeds shape up very well, both in protein and carbohydrate percentages. They contain plenty of Protein and the smallest percentages of Carbohydrate. Unfortunately, in all food there is Natural Fat and the Oil Seeds contain the most! For example, Beans and Peas contain 1.2 per cent and 1.1 per cent respectively; Maize has 4.5 per cent; Wheat 1.9 per cent; Barley 1.5 per cent; Dari 3.8 per cent; Rice 0.5 per cent; Oats 4.9 per cent. Compare the above Fat contents with Hemp 32 per cent, Linseed 36.5 per cent and Rape 55 per cent. Obviously, if the Oil Seeds are included in a pigeon's diet (and they should not be) one would have to be very careful of the amounts of seed included in it.

I have conducted many experiments with pigeon feeding in an effort to discover the best combination, and the weight of food, needed to maintain a racing pigeon in a good state of health. This work revealed that the protein and carbohydrate percentages, although important, are by no means critical. What is critical in all diets is the amount of Vitamins (and the range of vitamins) that is made available to the bird at every meal. Second only to the importance of the Vitamin is the Mineral content.

What is a Vitamin? It is a substance which although not a food acts as a catalyst of food. This vitaminic catalyst so acts upon food that it converts it to a condition in which the body can extract the true nutritional elements in the diet. If no vitamins, or if the vitamins are present in an inadequate quantity, then the food would pass through the bird's digestory tract without releasing any nourishment into the blood stream. Consequently, although free to swallow much food, the body would starve to death. I know that the picture of a pigeon with a full crop dying of malnutrition appears ludicrous yet this tragedy frequently happens in the lofts. Polyneuritis and Coccidiosis are two diseases which kill pigeons by starving them to death. The former is caused by vitamin deficiency in the diet while the latter is caused by an internal parasite. Thousands upon thousands of racing pigeons die every year from Polyneuritis purely because fanciers will not study pigeon diets in an attempt to learn how to give racing pigeons proper diets.

As I have stated above, grass (which grows the grains I have listed as Cereals) is sparse in vitamin content so that grain diets cannot be accepted as ideal for racing pigeons, especially as the animal's demand for vitamins is very great.

THE DIET

A very important vitamin and one that is needed to stimulate growth and power the restoration of body tissue is Vitamin 'A'. No athlete, and no racing pigeon, can thrive unless it can ingest sufficient Vitamin 'A' and 'D'. Beans and peas, which are very rich in Protein and contain less Carbohydrate than the Cereals, contain no Vitamin 'A'. How can racing pigeons fed on beans or peas alone thrive and develop 'racing form'? If fed on these legumes alone they would be permanently deprived of Vitamin 'A' and 'D'.

Nor is the alternative a mixture of Legumes and Cereal grains. 'Pigeon Mixtures', as they are called, stem from antiquity itself and in my youth, when little was known about vitamins and minerals, or about dietry itself, nearly every fancier bought commercially compounded 'mixtures' or mixed his own. Since then, two world wars and an appalling amount of human misery have taught us a great deal about the part played by Vitamins and Minerals in animal and human dietry, so much, in fact, that fanciers who ignore such matters are depriving themselves of any hope of success.

Maize contains a small amount of Vitamin 'A' as do deep-green peas. All grain is poor in Vitamin 'D' (practically nil) but most grains contain some of the water soluble 'B' Vitamins. Only one grain contains any Vitamin 'B.12' (the most important of the vitamins) and that is Linseed. Fortunately for racing pigeons, they don't need any Vitamin 'C' because they are able to convert their own from food.

According to information received from 'Old Hand' who keeps statistics gathered from his huge incoming mail from fanciers, 80 per cent of all pigeon ailments and diseases are caused by vitaminic deficiencies in the bird's diet (One Eyed Cold, Polyneuritis, etc.). This indicates that we have all got a lot to learn about pigeon dietry.

A long study of pigeon dietry reveals that a pigeon will deliberately over-eat of any grain other than the Tic Bean (Vicia Faba). The effect of over-eating is disastrous to the bird's potential as a racer. It becomes bloated and won't fly, even at exercise.

It is impossible for anyone to state exactly how much food should be issued as a ration to racing pigeons because, like human beings, appetites and bodily needs vary considerably. Size is no criterion. Like human beings, some of the largest eat less than some of the small ones. I stopped my birds from over-eating by putting hoppers before them charged with Tic Beans. In fact, I invited them to over-eat this grain. What happened? I never found a bird in the loft with more than half a crop of beans! It is not true to say that pigeons don't like Tic Beans. They do! Yet they seem to prefer grains that confer less benefit to them. They will only eat as many beans as they think they need. When I charged the hoppers with mixed grains every bird in the loft over-ate and a number became crop-bound. As I have said above, the Tic Bean is an ideal food for the racing pigeon but for notable defects. It contains no Vitamin 'A' which is absolutely necessary to a racing pigeon, and no Vitamin 'B.12' which is the only vitamin that can stall off and conquer Anaemia.

A pigeon who over-eats suffers pain as well as discomfort and the after effects of over-eating (excess fat). Pigeons eat before they drink. Thus, a crop packed full of grain has to try and accommodate soaked grain which swells to double its former, dry size. Birds in this condition would need to vomit in order to relieve the pain they are suffering but, strangely enough, a pigeon in this condition rarely vomits, nor is it easy for one to make it vomit. In most cases the only way of relieving the bird is to open its crop by making a surgical, vertical cut in it. This should be done with a sterilised (boiled) safety razor blade and the vertical cut should be made high in the crop, not low. The cut should be about $\frac{3}{4}$ inch long. The bird feels no pain from the surgery. After relieving the crop, sew the cut by inserting sutures (stiches) every $\frac{1}{4}$ inch of the cut.

Pigeons need clean water before them all day long. Nothing knocks a pigeon off form quite so much and so quickly as foul drinking water. In warm summer days the drinking water must be changed at least three times per day. Further, it should not be stood in a light place, only in a darkened spot because if water is exposed to much light, slime forms quicker than in water that is shaded, or darkened. It is not good enough for you to 'top' up the drinker. First tip out its water content then use a brush, or a rag to scrub out its interior. Then refill with fresh tap-water.

Incidentally, don't use a watering can. After a while the inside of the pouring tube collects filth and fouls up. This means that clean tap-water is fouled before ever it is poured into the drinker.

'Old Hand' carried out tests which proved that a pigeon drinks an average of $\frac{1}{8}$th of a pint of water per day, except when feeding youngsters, when it will need much more.

No fancier is entitled to expect his birds to work well and win if they do not receive Vitamin 'A' and 'D'. These vitamins are in the group 'A' 'D' 'E' and 'G', otherwise known as the Oil Soluble Group. Their best source is Cod Liver or Halibut Oil. Vitamin 'A' can also be got from Carotene, an orange agent.

Vitamin 'A' is also available in some greenstuffs (but not many). Few greenstuffs are suitable for feeding to racing pigeons. The greens have to be of a very dark colour to contain any vitamins. Watercress and mustard are in this category but cabbage and lettuce are useless.

Vitamin 'D', the vitamin for laying down Calcium and Phosphorus in the bones, is urgently needed by young pigeons for whom it helps to develop the skeletal frame. Vitamin 'D' is present in the above Liver Oils in plenty. Incidentally, the supply of these Oils must not be over-done. One result of an overdose would be the keratinisation of growing feather.

The Vitamin 'B' Group is extensive but vital to the racing pigeon's health. Important among this group are Thiamine (B.1), Riboflavin (B.2), Nicotinic Acid and B.12. There are seven others known as Folic Acid, Pyridoxine, Pantothenic Acid, Biotin, Choline, Paramino-benzoic Acid and Inositol.

Thiamine is soluble in water but is destroyed by Alkali (salt) so no fancier should use Epsom Salts or Bicarbonate of Soda in the loft. Thiamine functions in the body as a kind of governor for the release of energy from the Carbohydrates in food (the action of a catalyst). If Thiamine is absent from the diet the growth of nestlings will be checked and birds will start to go down with Polyneuritis. Birds who are excessively addicted to fighting, irritability and quarrelsomeness are betraying signs of Polyneuritis. The amount of Thiamine needed in the diet is proportional to the number of Calories provided by any nutrient, other than Fat. In order to utilise 100 Cal. from Carbohydrate, or Protein, the pigeon's body needs 0.04 of Thiamine. Just calculate the number of calories in the diet and multiply 100 by 0.04.

In the brewing of beer Barley is mashed in water, sugar is added and the mixture is fermented by Yeast. Yeast, which is a living organism, absorbs Thiamine from the grain. It is for this reason that Brewer's Yeast is a good source of this vitamin of the 'B' Group. However, Brewer's Yeast does not absorb Nicotinic Acid, nor Riboflavin, to the same extent as beer so this national beverage is an excellent food for human beings. Thiamine is A MUST for racing pigeons.

Riboflavin is a yellowy substance which gives off a green fluorescence in solution. It is soluble in water and can be destroyed by heat and ultra-violet rays. Its function is to form a link in the chain of processes by which the body obtains energy from food. A deficiency of Riboflavin in the diet checks the growth of youngsters and brings about cracks and sores in the region of the mouth and misting of the eyes. There is one very obvious, tell-tale symptom of a Riboflavin shortage in the diet, the pigeon's tongue turns the colour of magenta. It also develops a soreness. Most riboflavin is extracted from the liver but there is some in Brewer's Yeast.

Nicotinic Acid is another of the essential vitamins of the 'B' Group. Once Nicotinic Acid gets into the body it is converted into its proper form, Nicotinamide. It is also formed from one of the Amino Acids, Tryptophan. Nicotinic Acid functions to form another link in the chain of processes by which the body obtains energy from food.

Watch your young birds and be on the look-out for the sign of Nicotinic Acid deficiency in the diet. The bird's skin becomes red and rough, the tongue becomes sore and the digestion is upset so that diarrhoea occurs. Birds also suffer some mental disorder by appearing to be confused.

Racing pigeons fed only on an all-grain diet are bound to suffer from a range of ailments and diseases derived from vitaminic deficiencies but I think that few or none are likely to suffer from a deficiency of Folic Acid (regarded as a growth vitamin for young bodies).

Perhaps the most important of all the 'B' Group vitamins is the B.12. It is the most recently discovered of the 'B' Group of vitamins

THE DIET 93

and unlike all the other vitamins, it contains a metal – Cobalt. This very valuable Vitamin prevents the development of pernicious anaemia. When highly concentrated, B.12 re-energises pigeons and gives them a remarkable boost to their well-being, as well as holding at bay the dreaded anaemia which is rife in pigeon lofts. Above I have listed all the vital vitamins pigeons need and which must always be present in their day to day diet.

Earlier in this chapter I mentioned the importance of minerals in a pigeon diet. It is not generally known that in order to keep well and fit a pigeon needs access to some nineteen different kinds of minerals. All of these minerals must be extracted by the bird itself from the food it swallows.

Why do pigeons need such a wide range of minerals? (1) Because certain minerals help the body to grow. For example, the skeletal frame, claws, beak and feather are created out of minerals that include Calcium, Phosphorus and Magnesium. (2) Blood cells. The blood and flesh (muscles) and organs it builds and maintains need many minerals including Iron, Phosphorus and Sulphur. (3) Body stability. Salts bring stability to body fluids and they include the minerals Potassium, Sodium, Chlorine. (4) Energy reactions. When energy is released, as in the act of flying, Iron, Phosphorus and Manganese.

Other minerals also play their part. Copper, together with iron, makes blood cells. Iodine is part of the substance in the Thyroid Gland which helps control the expenditure of energy used up by the body. Cobalt has been traced in the anti-pernicious anaemia factor present in the Liver.

The absence of salt from the diet causes muscular cramp, mostly in the legs. The pigeon's skeleton, beak, claws and plumage are wholly dependent on a ready and steady supply of Calcium Phosphate and Phosphorus. This makes the mineral Calcium absolutely vital to a racing pigeon. Apart from this mineral's contribution to the bones and their structure it also effects the normal clotting of the blood and enables muscles to function properly.

One of the evils of allowing racing pigeons to over-eat, or eat fat-making foods, is that the fat gets into the intestine where, by acting as a kind of insulator, it can prevent the body from absorbing calcium from the food. Calcium is so important to the body that it is actually introduced into white bread (14 ounces to the 280 pound bag of flour).

You cannot supply Iron to your pigeons by putting metal, rusty or otherwise, such as nails, horse shoes, etc., in the drinking water. The birds derive iron from food alone, in the process of digestion. About three-quarters of the Iron found in a pigeon's body is stored in its blood where it is vital to the transportation of Oxygen to the tissues.

Once 'stocked up' with Iron the body loses it very slowly, almost imperceptibly. The Iron is contained in the haemoglobin in the red corpuscles and they have a life of about six weeks. When the six weeks expire the red corpuscles break up and the Iron is released. This released Iron does not escape from the body but is taken up and used in the creation of new red corpuscles. A result of Iron deficiency is Anaemia.

The most important element to a racing pigeon is Oxygen, a gas, because it is from this inhalant that the bird extracts most of its energy. It is known that some energy is extracted from food but the amount is tiny by comparison with the inhalant. A bird suffering from Respiratory Disease is not going to fill its Air Sacs (from which it breaths) and its lungs with energy-making Oxygen when its breathing system is impaired. Only a very fit pigeon can take full advantage of the free Oxygen of the air.

As I said above, another source of energy is Carbohydrate in the food intake and this is a compound of Carbon, Hydrogen and Oxygen, otherwise known as Starch, Cellulose and related substances. There are three kinds of Monosaccharides (simple sugars) in Carbohydrates. (1) Glucose, which is made from Starch, or by splitting more complex sugar, such as Sucrose. It occurs naturally in the blood of living animals and in the fruit and plant juices and plays a very important role in the life of the body. (2) Fructrose, from cane sugar and it can be changed into Glucose. (3) Galactose, which is part of the Lactose molecule. Starch represents no less than 50 per cent of the solid food of grain.

Much of the Starch in the daily diet provides heat but it is a fact, and one I deprecate, that the real end product of Carbohydrate is Fat, fat that congregates in the heart cavity and interior

THE DIET 95

body surfaces. When it has choked up the interior cavities it builds up on exterior body surfaces to weigh down the bird and interfere with and impede its physical functioning.

In the old days a fancier tossed down a few handfuls of grain and so far as he was concerned the problem of his birds' dietry was solved and satisfied. Poultry was also given a few handfuls of grain, on the ground, so that it scratched for it. It is only in the light of modern discovery that we realise (most of us for the first time) that dietry, even for farm or athletic animals, is more complex than we had imagined.

Some heedless fanciers (alleged to be 'of the old school') members of a rapidly diminishing out-moded cult, who blunder on as mere slaves to an ill-founded tradition, still throw down a mixture of grain and kid themselves that they are giving their birds a proper diet. The New Starter, however, has not fallen into the bad old ways. Raised in a world of technocrats he does not discount science and its forward-march. Instead, he wants to use science for his own advantage. What dad used to do is all right for dad. The son lives as a member of a new generation which, far from wanting to imitate dad, feels compelled to regard dad's world as an old-fashioned and redundant one, one which is out of step with what has now become modern practice. Consequently, he wants to do what is right today and not what appeared to be right twenty thirty, forty years ago.

Some of us had to live to become old men before we saw Neil Armstrong step out of his Moon Module and walk on the surface of the moon on July 20th, 1969. My father would have dismissed the Moon landing project as pure science fiction and nothing else. He would not have believed that the moon landing was practical. So, with modern progress in mind, the beginner doesn't rush around to the Corn Chandler and stock up with mixed grains for his birds. Instead, he sits down to study 'modern practice' and learn the most up-to-date methods of feeding pigeons.

The only grain I would ever give to racing pigeons is the Tic Bean. In fifty years my birds have never seen any other kind of grain except one. I know that the Tic Bean contains no vitamin 'A' and 'D' and that like all other grains it is short of this and that which the pigeon really needs. But a pigeon has a crop and

I think he ought to use it, hence the bean feeding. Yet, and here it is, I supplement the bean feeding by giving the birds a 'boost' supplement. In the first place, I know, as the result of my experiments, that my birds will not over-eat of the beans. They will eat just what they need. The 'boost' will give them what the bean cannot, the necessary vitamins and minerals to ensure good health and racing form. As I am not writing this book for advertising purposes I refuse to put a name to the 'boost' and other specifics which keep your birds on their toes, such descriptions can be found elsewhere.

The effect of a scientific 'boost' on racing pigeons has to be seen to be believed! After some 7–14 days of feeding 'boost' the condition of the birds staggers the imagination! Many an 'old hand' who always fed his birds on a mixture of grain has been known to jump out of his shoes when he saw the effect of 'boost' on his racing pigeons. It is one of those things that can be seen to happen.

Birds fed on grain-only diets are no match for those raised and trained on 'boost'. Never listen to any fancier who claims big performances for birds fed on grain alone. Every fancier has his 'secret' although few care to reveal them, for obvious reasons.

There remains but one more item in connection with a pigeon's diet that I have to mention. It is the bird's grit. Pigeons always take up a little grit. You can waste your money on proprietary brands if you wish. All my birds are given is the sharp sand of the deep litter on which they live. If I didn't use deep litter in the loft compartments I would let the birds pick up what grit they needed in the garden and, if they were prisoners, I would place a small turf in a box and put it in the loft for them. I think that fanciers who actually pay money for grit must be millionaires, with money to burn. Most pigeons ingest their food without recourse to grit of any kind and of all those necessities our birds demand, grit is about the most meaningless.

The Oil Seeds (Hemp, Linseed, etc.) must never become part of a diet. Hemp and Linseed, mixed in equal proportions, make up a Seed Mix which is used only as a tit-bit, a coax to tempt birds to trap quickly. It must be given to the birds very sparingly, about as much as will cover a new penny piece, per pigeon, per day.

It would not be possible for a fancier of experience to conclude

THE LOFT END
This view of the loft shows the tall louvre-panel which is inserted in that part of the loft which is the end of the front corridor. Another similar panel is installed in the opposite end wall. (*See* chapter One)

FRONT CORRIDOR
View of one half of the front Corridor taken from the Trapping corridor. Note row of louvre panels just above floor level on left. The wire-screened windows are also fitted with transparent plastic sheeting stretched on frames. These frames are hinged at top but are held at bottom with a hinged stay. The stay holds the window open during the summer, thus adding another louvre-effect to the ventilation. It is lowered and closed in winter. Above, along the ceiling, continuous strip-lighting has been installed. The drinkers stand in this corridor and birds reach through the compartment wall which is dowelled. Beside each Drinker stands a plastic hopper while on the right of the drinker is an electric power-point into which is plugged 2 strip lights. This lighting circuit is governed by a thermostat which brings the lights on over the drinkers when the air temperature falls to 35°F to prevent drinking water from freezing. The floor of the Corridor is tiled with PVC tiles to make the floor inhospitable to the Cocci-worm and the Trichomonais germ. (*See* chapter One)

THE TRAPPING CORRIDOR

The view is of the Trapping Corridor with sliding doors open. The Front corridor runs away on either side, the full length of the loft (75ft) The opening into the Front Corridor on either side of the Trapping Corridor closed by a pair of hinged doors on either side. In the picture can be seen the sliding door that opens into the first loft compartment on the left. At the rear of the Trapping Corridor is a pair of hinged doors which lead into a storeroom at the rear of the loft. Normally, this pair of doors would close a cupboard with shelf for timing clock, etc. When the race bird pitches into the Trapping Corridor it is only necessary to draw the sliding doors to close behind one while one bends down to pick up the bird and relieve it of its race rubber. The floor of the loft about 12 in. above ground level. This floor is also covered with PVC tiles to render the surface inhospitable to parasites. (*See* chapter One)

THE LOFT

View of the Weybridge Loft which is an example of multiplication of units giving twelve internal compartments plus the Trapping Corridor which is closed by two sliding doors. The white panels along front both below and above windows are louvred for ventilation. The dowels in front windows are for ornamentation only, fine mesh wire screens have been fixed behind them to keep out wild birds. (*See* chapter One)

THE BIG VEE PERCH

The illustration is of three panels of home-made Big Vee perches. The Big Vees are fixed to a strip of timber or plastic and nailed to the loft wall. These particular perches were cut from chip-board (bonded with phenol plastic) and screwed together. The two wings of the Big Vee are 12in. long and 6in. wide and they are spaced approximately 14in. apart. (*See* chapter Two)

A PIGEON NESTBOWL

This is an earthenware nestbowl standing in its own metal bowl. It is a continental production and we believe that the metal bowl is supposed to discourage parasites from crawling into the nest. (*See* chapter Two)

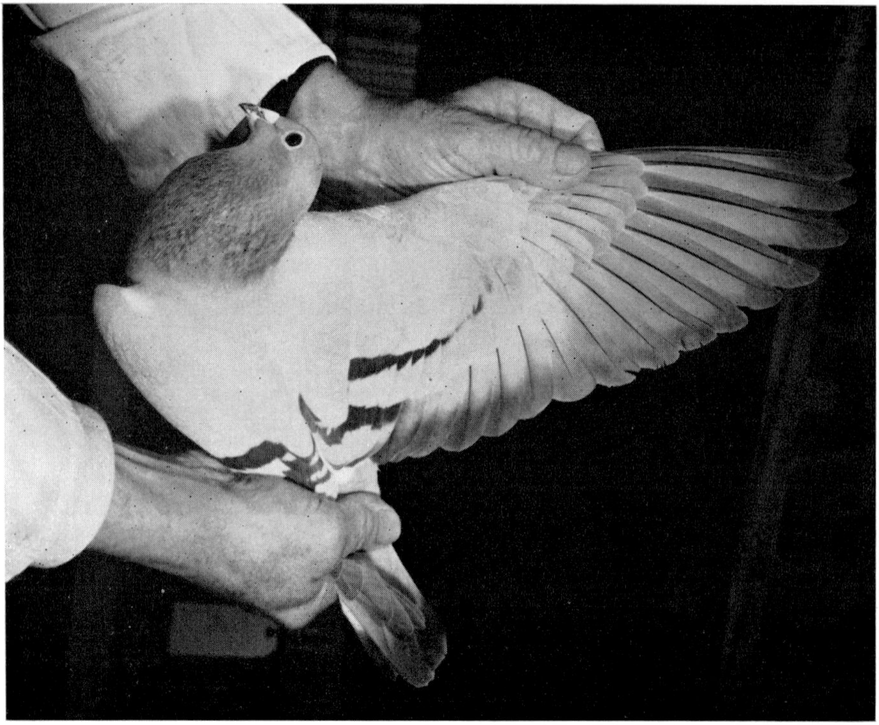

THE RACING PIGEON'S WING
Shows how a racing pigeon's wing is 'spanned' by pulling on the roots of the outside flights where they grow from the wing. Note that there are Ten Primary Flights. The Secondary flights, which are of a different shape, follow on from the Primary Flights. (*See* chapter Four)

A FEATHER ABNORMALITY
This pigeon feather grew another from the quill of the proper feather. This is an abnormality which must not be encouraged. (*See* chapter Four)

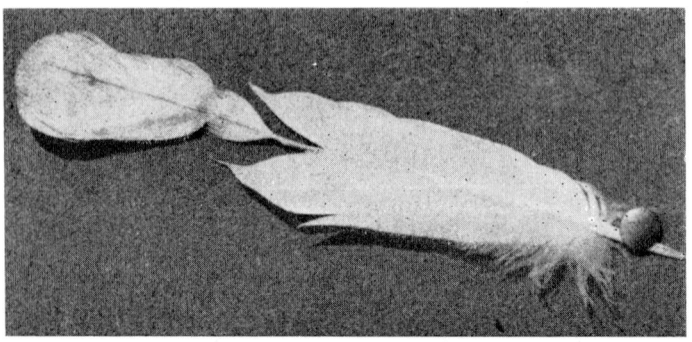

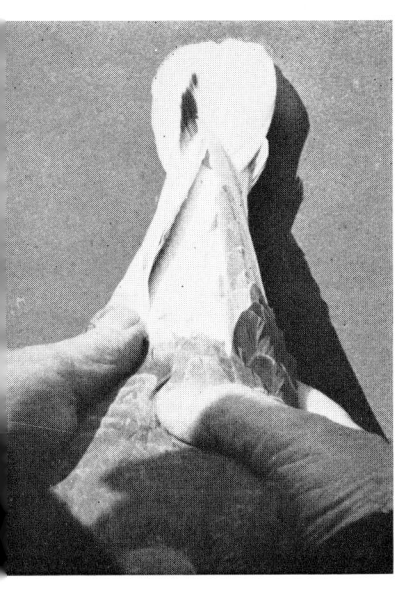

THE RUMP
The thumb of the right hand is pressing down on the bird's rump. Note how the tail feathers appear as one. Note, too, the distance between the end of the flights of the folded wing and the tip of the tail. (*See* chapter Four)

THE RACING PIGEON'S TAIL
The fanned tail in the picture carries twelve feathers known as the 'Tail Rectrices' which grow and moult in pairs, numbered as shown. (*See* chapter Four)

TRUE DESCENT
The Blue Chequer Shearing-Logan Cock who is Reference 'A' in the Stud Book of S. & D. Bishop of Weybridge. He was a g-son of both 'Champion 1826' (J. W. Logan's Red Chequer Hen and winner of the King's Cup from San Sebastian, Spain) and 'Champion 69' (J. W. Logan's 9th Open Grand National San Sebastian race) The Blood of 'True Descent' runs in that of every bird in the Weybridge Loft today. (*See* chapter Four)

A PIGEON RACING TIMING CLOCK
Timing clocks are specially designed and made for pigeon racers. The model portrayed is a Benzing Comatic. (*See* chapter Three)

THE 'BENT' KEEL
The picture is of the Sternum (Breast) Bone, otherwise known as 'The Keel,' of a racing pigeon. Instead of being straight the bone has 'waved'. This is known as 'Bent Keel' or 'a wave in the keel.' It occurs at the time the bird hatches from its shell and is a sign of skeletal weakness. (*See* chapter Four)

THE ROCK DOVE
(Columba Livea)
All modern racing pigeons are descendants of the wild Rock Dove, a native of this country of a specie that does not emigrate. Note the pearl eye and shape of head with its short, thick beak, small wattle and eye-cere. (*See* chapter Four)

THE PIGEON'S NEST
A Blue Hen (blue wing with two black bars) is seen sitting on the nest she has made in the corner of her nestbox. The nesting material is mainly transported to the nestbox by the cock to be loosely woven into a nest by the hen. (*See* chapter Five)

RINGING A SQUEAKER
A metal registration ring must be slipped onto the leg of a squeaker before its seventh day of age. These metal rings are supplied by the member's Union and each has a code and serial number which is recorded in the Unions' Ring Register. As the squeaker's claws grow and set it is not possible to remove the metal ring except by cutting it through. By referring to its Ring Register Union officials can trace the ownership of every racing pigeon that bears a metal ring on its leg. (*See* chapter Five)

THE GROWING WING
Below: Note the growth of the feathers in this spanned squeaker's wing. The feathers can be seen shooting from their sheaths. (*See* chapter Five)

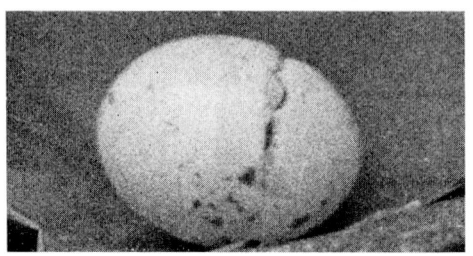

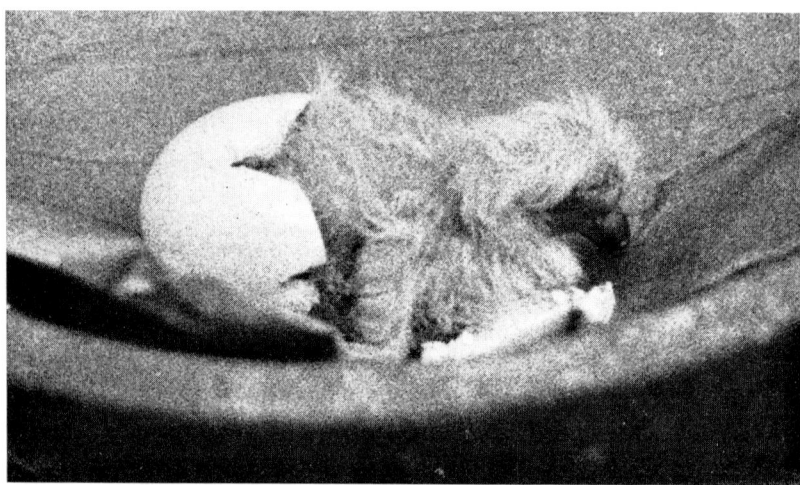

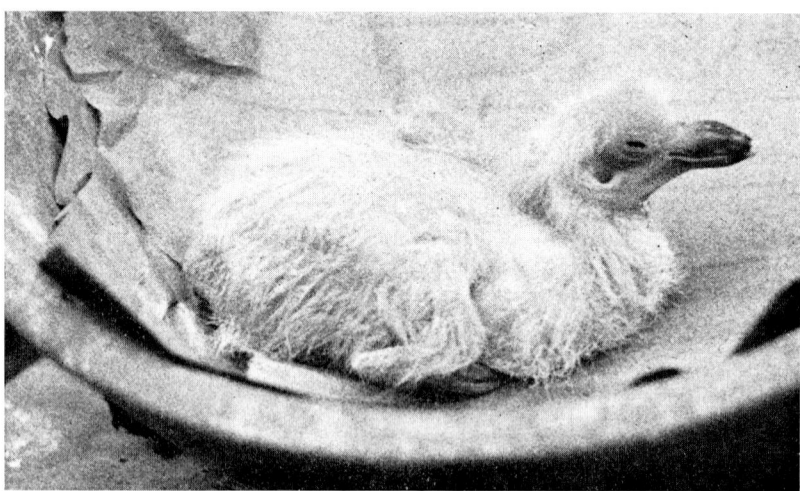

HATCHING OF A SQUEAKER

(1) The chipping egg. (2) The hatching squeaker emerging from the shell. (3) The squeaker in its nestbowl. Note that the squeaker's body is amply covered with yellow 'down' (hairs) All healthy hatched squeakers are well covered with hairy down. (*See* chapter Five)

THE RACE RINGING
One member of the race marking committee is holding a pigeon's leg to the ringing machine while another member operates the lever which shoots a rubber ring, printed with serial numbers, onto the leg of the pigeon. The official standing behind the fancier holding the pigeon is getting ready to rubber stamp the bird's wing with the club secretary's name and address. (*See* chapter Nine)

A WEST COUNTRY PIGEON SHOW
A West Country show staged by the late Reg Nicholls, President of the great West of England Amalgamation. The Red Chequer Hen *Per Ardua* is the 'Gibraltar Hen (1,098-miles) and 'Ruhr Express' is the Dicken Medal winner, both the property of the author.

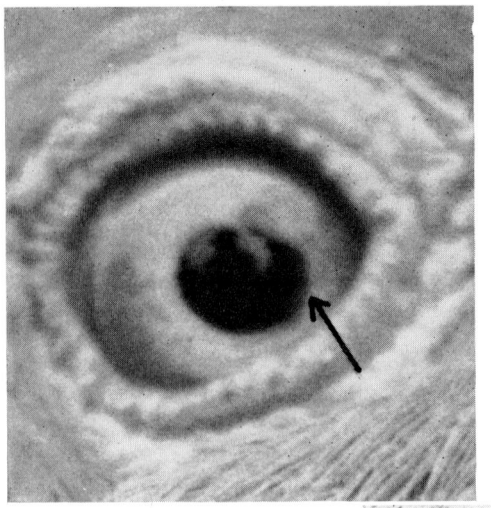

The EYE SIGN
The arrow, right bottom of the picture, points to the dark marking which is known as 'a standing sight' of Eye-Sign. (*See* chapter Eleven)

ONE EYED COLD
Note how the feather in the region of the eye gets soaked with moisture from the watery eye of the bird suffering from One Eyed Cold. One Eyed Cold should not be confused with the watery eye of a bird that has been pecked in a quarrel. The difference between the two is indicated when the water laying in the lower lid is seen to contain tiny air bubbles, the symptom of One Eyed Cold. (*See* chapter Thirteen)

WEBBED FEET
The picture illustrates an abnormality because racing pigeons should not be web-footed. (*See* chapter Thirteen)

LOADING A ROAD TRANSPORTER

The Road Transport is the property of the West of England South Road Combine and it is in the process of being loaded. Picture No. 2 shows the specially constructed wooden crate in which the birds are carried. (*See* chapter Sixteen)

A RACE LIBERATION
The picture shows the simultaneous liberation of racing pigeons from the West Yorkshire Federation's Road Transporter. (*See* chapter Sixteen)

a chapter on the art of feeding without pointing out that young birds may not be fed in the same way as old birds. Old birds will respond satisfactorily if given the open hopper. Young birds will not.

Until a youngster becomes wing strong (able to fly up to a perch) it must be given all it can eat and more. It is in the initial hatching weeks that the bird is made, so let it have ample supplies of a good, nourishing diet. Once it can use its wings to fly it must be put onto a hard and fast ration. I am being very serious about this so please take special note.

When the youngsters begin to fly give them a daily ration of $\frac{1}{2}$ ounce of tic beans plus the standard measure of boost, in the afternoon, after they have had their period of exercise. No more until next day!

The old practice of letting birds out for a morning and evening toss, with food after each bout of exercise, is not recommended. Ideally, let the youngsters out only once per day, at the most suitable time which, if you are out at work all day, should be in the evening. They must go out with an empty crop and fly. After they return from exercise they should be given their beans and 'boost' and get no more until they repeat the performance next day. When they are put out for training, feed exactly as described in the chapter on Training. Do not allow anyone to persuade you to treat them differently. Stick to what I have recommended and you will get the best results.

VII

Training Youngsters, Yearlings and Old Birds

Keeping racing pigeons involves a fancier in two separate forms of labour: (1) That work which he carries out in his loft by way of pigeon maintenance, keeping of records, etc.; (2) The work of training the pigeons along the line-of-flight. In my experience, most fanciers are prepared to shape up to the work of maintenance but most of the back-sliding occurs when the time comes for road-training the birds.

What every new starter must bear in mind is that all athletes must undergo the work and the disciplines of training. The principle reason for drawing up strict training schedules is to subject the athlete to a course of action, otherwise known as a routine, which is calculated to contribute to the advancement of the athlete's health and skill.

Athletes run, jump, cycle, or kick a ball around for hours every day, under the direction of an expert, for the special purpose of developing the body and the mind to adjust to the strain of performance and the pressure of competition. No matter whether the athlete is human, racehorse, greyhound, or racing pigeon, it can only excel in that performance for which it is a candidate if it trains its mind and body to master the technique of its chosen sport.

Certain qualities are necessary in an athlete, or athletic animal, which do not figure in the life of a domestic animal or pet. These are physical and mental. Athletes must be strong and very healthy. Any bodily weakness or mental mal-adjustment prohibits performance. Therefore, to a certain extent, talent or flair is essential. However, the possession of aptitude, important though it may be, only gives the athlete a start. It cannot become a champion unless it is taught the vital technique of using its powers to its best advantage. This applies as much to racing pigeons as to all other athletic performers.

No man should keep racing pigeons unless he is prepared and able to train them. Many keep pigeons and 'jump' them untrained into the races, hoping that they will stay with the 'drag' and be accompanied back home but these fanciers only put up the money for more industrious members to win.

The new starter's first task is to come to grips with what training is all about and what it is not. For instance, we do not train pigeons along the line-of-flight so that they can refresh their memories with the sight of the course and its landmarks. The truth is that racing pigeons need no geography lessons. Like almost everything else they do, they navigate by instinct, so there is nothing we can teach them about routes and roads, aerial or otherwise.

If a pigeon finds itself flying towards a hill it will make no attempt to raise its ceiling of flight so that it can pass over it. Instead, it turns to left or right and flies round the hill. If you toss a pigeon from the top of a hill it will promptly drop down to the valley below. It is not grateful to you for liberating it at a great height so that it can see its way to a more distant horizon because it is quite uninterested in it. Watch trainees and racers homing in an East wind. They hop over hedges and fly as low as possible in order to put an obstacle between themselves and the East wind. At such low ceilings they see only a short distance ahead but plod unerringly on their way home. They know where they are going and they will arrive there if they have the will, the stamina and the luck. If your bird is homeward bound and it can see a rain-storm blowing-up ahead it will not fly on into the rain but will try and make a detour, thus skirting the deluge. It acts in this way because it is by no means a stupid and capricious bird but a very clever one.

If fanciers were to take less interest in teaching pigeons how to navigate and give more in providing them with vital muscle-exercise, through which the power of the wing is built up and toned, many members would achieve better results in the races.

Young pigeons that are fit and well are fairly bursting with energy. The energy they expend in their first aerial transports appears to be unlimited. See how they dash about in the sky before they learn to 'kit' and fly in a drag. Later, when they are exercised, they plod around the chimney pots in a circling flight which is referred to as 'exercise'.

It is not long before the wing-strong youngster takes to the air and flies strongly round the housetop and it is at this juncture that I put on record my first warning. Never let your youngsters out with old birds, even with yearlings! Exercise your old birds early on and get them in. Then let the youngsters out to exercise on their own.

The first thing you will notice is that youngsters tend to fly for much longer periods than old birds. After some twenty minutes of flying some old birds will want to drop and return to the loft where they have a nestbox, or perch, waiting for them. The youngsters will betray no such eagerness to re-enter the loft and if they are very fit they will not fly for less than an hour but often up to and in excess of two hours.

It would not do to let the youngsters take their exercise with the old birds because the young always imitate the old. Therefore, when the old birds soon tired of exercise and dropped they might bring the youngsters down with them. The strict rule must be that old bird and young bird exercise separately.

After a few weeks you will notice that the young birds are behaving somewhat strangely. They are beginning to 'range'. What is meant by this pigeon term? It means that instead of plodding round the housetops in circling flight the youngsters are clearing off, first in one direction across the sky to disappear and to reappear later from another direction, swiftly to disappear again in another. They keep up this 'ranging' for one to two hours or more.

You may not know it but this 'sky ranging' by your youngsters carries them over a twenty-mile radius of the home terrain (this has been proven).

I have calculated that when my youngsters start to range they fly from 60–100 miles a day (based on the pigeon's mean speed of 40 m.p.h.). Very few fanciers pause to consider the amount of work done by their youngsters around home every day of the week.

What is the direct result of all this day-work by youngsters? It is two-fold. Firstly, the work swells the muscles and develops them. Secondly, the work tends to enlarge the heart. All athletes develop hearts that are bigger than those of sedentary types. There is yet another advantage of importance. All pigeons are gregarious, which is to say that they flock together. In the course of their 'ranging' your youngsters will join batches of other pigeons, especially those who are exercising around the housetops of local fanciers. Naturally, your little lot will join up with others as they race across the sky but they will know when to break away and return home. Their early lessons in 'breaking away' will stand them in good stead when they start work along the line-of-flight.

Here is yet another warning. If your youngsters have not started to range by the time you wish to start them on road-work, you are in dead trouble. Never start to train youngsters until they have 'ranged' for several weeks.

Supposing the youngsters refuse to range? What then? The first thing you should ask yourself is 'why not?' If the youngsters are well bred and very healthy, with empty crops, they should 'range' automatically. If they do not you must suspect that something is wrong with them. They ail, or they are too fat. If they are not ranging by eight weeks of age begin working on them to try and find out what is stopping them from taking a natural course.

What is likely to happen if you start them along the road before they have ranged? Losses, big, heart-breaking losses will overtake your team. I write from long experience. Whenever I have tried to train 'unranged' youngsters I have sustained the kind of losses which make even the strongest want to weep. Whole teams have been wiped out simply because the youngsters have not learned to break-away from aerial company.

During the 'ranging' youngsters explore miles and miles of country around the loft in all compass directions. This helps them when they are carried over 'the top' on race days. When I refer to my training register (I keep records of all training tosses) I find that from four teams, totalling in all in excess of forty youngsters, only one was lost in the course of over forty training tosses before the programme opened. That was because those youngsters 'ranged'. In another year, when for a reason I found unaccountable at the time, the youngsters refused to range I lost more than 50 per cent of the total number before the first young bird race was reached.

Old birds don't range. Fanciers think they do but in most cases when they are out of sight they are down in some farmer's field, fielding.

Traditionally, most fanciers exercise their birds morning and evening. I do not. My birds are given one daily exercise period (late afternoon) and that is all. This means that they are given one meal a day, after they have trapped into the loft from their exercise flight. It is essential that young birds shall not be turned out to fly while they still have corn in the crop, hence my one daily exercise period.

Our basic requirement of the pigeon is that it shall fly fast and straight to its home loft. Not that it shall fly ornamentally, as one of a batch of tired and bored pigeons who merely circle the loft every day. Remember, fast and straight for home.

It is a fact that all performing animals must be taught to run or fly straight since by nature they crave to weave, or move in circles. It is for this reason that young racehorses must be run upsides (alongside experienced racehorses) to teach them how to run straight, something which is not in their nature. The responsibility for teaching young pigeons to fly straight-line rests firmly on the shoulders of the novice.

Remember, too, that the only animals one can teach to do anything at all are the very youngest. There is only one time to learn and that is when the mind is not cluttered up with adult experiences and reactions.

The time to start your youngsters schooling along the road is when their mauve baby eye changes its colour to the adult iris coloration. This usually occurs when the youngster is ten weeks old. At that age all 'ten-weekers should be placed in a training pannier and locked in. On one side of the pannier fix a water trough and on the other a trough containing a little food. It is imperative that your youngsters be taught not to fear the pannier. Give them a day and a night in the pannier and then liberate them from it in the garden outside your loft. After three such sessions they should be ready for road work. Incidentally, even at this young age it is necessary to separate cocks from hens in the basket.

The first road toss should be quite near home. I would suggest from one to two miles. I know that the youngsters have ranged round the loft for distances upward of and probably in excess of twenty miles. So why start them at only one or two miles? Well, we are committed to a policy of teaching the youngsters to fly a straight line so this is the best way of doing it.

Once your youngsters are committed to the line of flight they are exposed to the hazard of aerial clashing with other pigeons being trained by other fanciers, attack by hawk, the trigger-happy gunman, low flying aircraft, cables and wire stretched across their line of flight, etc. These are the natural hazards but there are others. For instance, in almost every new team of youngsters there is at least one bird with the mind of an itinerant, a ubiquitous type who has no intention of returning home, probably because it believes that the hempseed will taste sweeter elsewhere.

It would be wrong for us to assume that our pigeons are so very, very different mentally from other animals of the kingdom of which we, too, are subjects. Some pigeons are energetic, some are lazy. This is plainly demonstrated at a time when the cocks are supposed to be busy fetching and transporting nesting material, so that their hens can construct a nest for their eggs to be laid in. Some cocks work hard and supply so much material that their hens are able to build a nest upwards of twelve inches high. Others weary of the task when the nests consist of no more than two or three twigs. Then there is the devious type who flatly refuses to fly and forage for his hen so that she can 'keep up' with the hen next door. Instead, he hangs about in the loft until a hard-working type sets off on another nesting-material search. Then he nips into the nestbox and steals the twigs which he then hands over to his hen, nor does he fail to bask in the gratitude all females bestow on hard-working husbands.

Incidentally, the cocks who work the hardest gathering nesting material are the ones most likely to put on early 'racing form'.

If you watch this energetic type you will find that it flies hundreds of miles on twig-finding expeditions.

You will breed birds of the kind that strike you as being intelligent and others, in greater numbers, who will convince you that they are as stupid as some humans you know and could name. No matter how blue-blooded your stock may be they are bound to breed what we call 'a fielder', viz. the sort of bird who is incapable of homing across a field without going down to peck it over. Farmers who don't know the difference between a wood pigeon and a racing pigeon, including those who do know but don't care, usually shoot these fielders. Then there is the cock with a roving eye for a passing hen and vice versa, the dawdler and the layabout. All types well known in human society and which are duplicated in the racing pigeon kingdom.

I recollect the time when I entered two birds in a 500-mile race. As I stood in the garden I saw two birds appear in the distance, flying side by side, obviously heading for my loft. I was delighted and thrilled. 'Fancy,' I said to myself, 'fancy my two entries flying together and racing each other home, over a distance of 500 miles! Fancy staying together over that long, long trail!'

The Red Chequer Cock shot into the Trapping Corridor of my loft and was quickly timed. Then I looked round for the other bird and saw it standing in the centre of the lawn. 'Strange,' I muttered to myself, 'our birds don't do that sort of thing.' I walked near the bird and found it to be a strange hen. While I watched her she trotted over to the garden pond, took a long drink and then treated herself to a bath. Some considerable time later, when she had dried off, she took to the air and disappeared along the route she had traversed to my house. If that hen was a competitor in the same race as my cock (and her leg sported a matching rubber) the owner was going to clock a very late pigeon.

When you find yourself with a few empty perches don't bother to strain your brain for the reason for their absence. After reading this chapter you can guess where they get to. In my young days it was firmly believed by most fanciers that their birds never really went missing, they only called in at other lofts where they were feloniously and spitefully trapped and kept for breeding purposes. The theory that other fanciers fiendishly coveted our pigeons and would willingly break Union Rules to hold on to them is a fallacy. Very few pigeons enter strange lofts. The vast majority of those birds who are lost every year (well over one million in this country) go feral (wild) and roost in barns, on farmhouses or, if they prefer an urban-like existence, they roost on steeples (steeple-sitters) or on city buildings. Never, never repine over your young bird losses.

All young birds who go missing are not necessarily useless pigeons but I regret that in the majority of cases the birds who become strays are useless. As a young lad I had a stray enter my loft and I reported it. The owner wrote to tell me he didn't want it back. If I would keep it he would send me five bob as a sweetener. I kept the bird, trained it, raced it, and won many prizes with it. Yet according to the breeder the bird was hopeless when trained to its home loft. Why? Some men work better and enjoy life more when they emigrate from Britain to work and live in Australia or Canada, for example. To some the grass is always greener on the other side of the hill. Undoubtedly, the stray that came into my loft liked it a great deal better than its own home loft because I never did lose it in a race. Inconsistencies of this kind make the sport even more interesting than it is.

There are two ways of losing youngsters. One is in training and racing. The other is in the dreaded 'Fly-away'. This tragedy occurs when the loft is over-crowded (too many youngsters on perches). The fly-away occurs when the youngsters conclude that there are too many of them in the loft. One summer morning, when the youngsters are turned out to exercise, they will 'kit' and fly towards the horizon. If you are around to see it you will soon know what has happened to you. Once the birds disappear over the horizon you will never see one of them again.

Too many lofts are too small. Alternatively, too many small lofts contain too many birds. Result, birds start to suffer from the Stress Syndrome and eventually they solve their problem in the only way they know, by clearing off to new feeding grounds.

You have no need to train 'round the loft' (from different compass points) if your youngsters range. Be careful about the 'line-of-flight'. This cannot be found by drawing a straight line on a map from racepoints to loft. The terrain must be taken into account.

I recommend you to consult a relief map from which you will discover that your birds fly a course that weaves through hill and dale and is much longer than the Great Circle measurement of the distance flown.

When training youngsters the important thing is not so much the line-of-flight as the number of tosses the youngsters receive. Personally, I toss every day if the weather is amenable. And I start tossing them in June. This means they are given six weeks of intensive training before the programme opens about the 1st of August. You are probably asking why I train so often and so hard? Firstly, I believe that young pigeons should be worked hard because this inculcates into them the discipline of working until it becomes a habit. Secondly, I learnt from experience that hard-worked youngsters produce the most winners. Fanciers who give their birds a few 'mid-week' tosses before racing begins and then just lift their birds into the races week by week get the kind of results they deserve. The object of racing is to win and one employs the very best system to this end.

Young trainees are controlled through their stomachs. This does not mean they are starved. When the youngsters return from the training toss or race they are given $\frac{1}{2}$ ounce of tic beans and then the standard ration of 'boost'. That is all but it is enough. The beans without the 'boost' would not be enough but the combination of bean and boost is plenty. With this kind of diet plus the 60/100 miles a day exercise you will find that their bodies harden up while the muscles swell. By the time tomorrow and its work period comes round they have emptied their crops and are ready to fly again. I have tried training youngsters with food in their crops with disastrous results. No athlete can work on a full or even half-full stomach and the same rule applies to young pigeons.

Cull those youngsters who do not respond to the system. Cull those who hang about the loft and will not exercise with the others. Watch the progress of the moult. It is unfortunate that the youngsters have to be raced when they are moulting but there is nothing we can do about it except ensure that no youngsters are sent away when there are bare patches on their bodies or large gaps in their tails.

It is preferable for you to divide up your youngsters into two teams for racing. Never put all your eggs in one basket, so to speak. In every race programme there is at least one 'smash', a day on which many of the birds are lost. If all your birds are engaged in this tragic event you will be gravely short of yearlings next season. Send one team this week and another next, thus gambling in numbers but observing some caution. The most prudent fancier is always the biggest winner.

Yearlings should be trained similarly to the youngsters with multiple tosses at reasonable distances because they are still only over-grown babies. After say ten tosses start them all over again but this time by single-tossing. This method requires you to toss a bird on its own and wait for some ten or fifteen minutes after it has cleared off before tossing another one. My method is to take a flask of tea, some sandwiches and a good book and drive to open but rural country to toss the birds single and at my ease. Please don't expect your yearlings to excel when matched against two-year-old birds and upwards. They still have a lot to learn before they can cope with the more experienced racers in the panniers. Yearlings fly no better on a ration so give them access to a hopper, the same as the older birds.

The third season bird, what we term 'a two-year-old' is a different kind of bird from the yearling and the youngster. He is no longer young, skittish and a bit silly but a bird whose body is nearing maturity and with two racing seasons behind him. That is a long time in a pigeon's life. He has probably flown thousands of miles and in all sorts of company. Further, after one season on the nest he will have a fixed idea of the kind of life he prefers to live. Being pulled off the nest every day for a training toss from a spot he knows well through sickening repetition is not the way of life he desires nor will he submit meekly to it.

Multiple tossing of two-year-olds and upwards does more harm than good. According to my records this sort of work tends to slow down the bird, exactly as the monotonous week-by-week racing stales the bird and drops its speed. I've known some old birds who were good yearling winners from 300 miles take a night out from a five-mile training toss as two-year-olds. That action constituted clear sulking and it was a warning to me. Naturally, I reacted by abandoning the daily multiple short distance toss.

Sitting on eggs or feeding youngsters is the two-year-old's true delight and it will begrudge every minute it has to spend away from its nestbox. However, even two-year-olds must be trained if their muscle is to be toned and they are to be brought to a state of fitness. This means they must work at training. Here one must arrive at a decision which in my case was to change the style of training. I decided that from the age of two years and upwards they would not be sent along the trail every day but only, say, twice a week. At the same time, they would be singled-up every time. My practice is to send these older birds to the first stage (25 miles) and then by long 'jumps' at 50 miles, 100 miles up to 200 miles per toss. An old bird flying, say, two 200-mile tosses per week is receiving as much work as he needs to keep fit. The longest single toss I have ever given a pigeon is 450 miles when I was flying the North Road from Scotland.

The value of single-up tossing becomes apparent when one competes in the 'classic' open events (National races, etc.). The drag isn't going to hold together for long in races open to the whole country so that what one really needs is a bird which is capable of pulling out of the drag and homing on its lonesome. I know that pigeons are gregarious but the only bird who is willing to fly alone is the one who has been trained not to fear being on its lonesome when in the air.

No fancier should try teaching two-year-olds and upwards to fly singly. The losses would be too great. Never leave it later than the yearling stage to teach the birds how to fly solo. As I said before, the only time to teach birds is when they are young.

Never persevere with the training of a youngster who 'plays about' and does not behave in a consistent manner. Cull as you go along. Sooner or later the youngsters undergoing training will 'break up' which is to say that their batch, or drag, will be broken up through aerial clashing with other birds so that your youngsters return singly. This happening is inevitable. However, take note of which birds return early and which late, with particular attention to those who turn up next day after spending a night on the tiles. Remember that what you are looking for are the consistent birds, the ones you can always rely upon because they will be the loft's true strength in years to come.

Young bird winners are not necessarily your best youngsters. In my experience young bird winners have not been my best long distance old birds. On the other hand, consistency is the criterion, even if the youngsters tended to be somewhat slow. So many novices get rid of the slower youngsters and keep only the fast ones yet the former might make the best long distance birds in future years.

IX

Pigeon Racing Techniques

While there are a number of 'systems' of racing pigeons most of them are variations of two well-known systems: (1) The Natural System; (2) The Widowhood System.

It is believed by most fanciers that it is natural for a racing pigeon to fly home to its loft, and the perch, and the nest it loves so much. Therefore, pigeons raced on the 'Natural System' live freely in the loft, with their mates, and carry on in the nest exactly as they would behave in the wild. Both cock and hen may be raced. I will describe the practice of this system, starting with the opening of the breeding season which, in so far as breeding from racers is concerned, will start normally at the end of the first week in March.

About a month before the birds are actually mated (7th/9th March) the sexes should be separated. Some fanciers separate the sexes long before this date but I have found that a month of separation is all that is necessary. In an 'open loft' (as I term the type described in Chaper One of this book) the birds are given no inducement to mate once winter comes on. The period of separation tends to make the birds keen to mate so they may be a little excited when restored to their mates but they should soon settle down. Try and choose a sunny day for the actual mating-up. All the racing pairs should be allowed to rear at least one youngster in the first nest of the season and then lay a second round. These eggs they may sit but not hatch out. Avoid hatching by substituting 'crock' eggs, or boil the eggs they are allowed to sit on. When swopping eggs under pigeons make sure the new ones you put under them (crocks, etc.) have been warmed beforehand. Sitting birds tend to desert chilled eggs.

When both cock and hen have been sitting about twelve days on eggs they will begin to make pigeon milk (curd) on their breasts which will build up until the nineteenth day when the eggs should hatch. This milk, or curd, is referred to as 'soft food'. It is believed by many that this is a bad time to race sitting pigeons whom, they say, should be stopped until the pigeon milk has dried up and the birds are back to their normal physical condition. It is also claimed that trouble is afoot for the bird who loses its nest after making soft food. The fact is that nothing untoward happens to the bird. It just stops making pigeon milk and the soft food condition dries up.

It will surely have occurred to you that if you mate up all your racers on the same day, or thereabouts (I refer to the birds you hope to race with) and if the hens all lay their eggs to time (eight days from day of mating) then they will all be sitting and making soft food on the 12th day from egg-laying! Fanciers racing their birds on the Natural System should 'stagger' the matings so that all the birds are not in the same condition on the same date.

Incidentally, I don't think it is a good thing to send both cock and mated hen to the same race point. I believe that the bird who is doing the racing is entitled to fly home and find his mate (or her mate) sitting in a warm nest. What is the alternative? Both birds returning to a cold, deserted nest with the eggs gone! This means re-mating so that by the time the following race weekend comes along the cock is driving madly and the hen is in egg, two conditions which could spoil the chances of either bird.

I suggest that the novice starts his Old Bird Racing season with his two-year-olds and upwards (if he has any) and keeps them going until the end of May. At this stage, stop the two-year-olds and engage the yearlings. Yearlings do not usually perform well until they have dropped their first primary flight which falls in early June. Thus, the yearlings fly the middle distance races while the older birds (if any) have a rest. When the longer distance races come along (about the third week in June) the yearlings are stopped for the season, or are engaged only in the shorter events which are sometimes staged in between the long races, while the older birds are 'jumped' into the long races which conclude the old bird season's programme.

A glance at your club's Old Bird programme will reveal that the events begin with a short race (about 70/90 miles) and from then onwards, week by week, the race distances gradually extend until the longer distances at 400, 500 and 600 miles are reached. Because the week-by-week races increase by distances of about 35-45 miles at a time, some novices believe that pigeons should not be asked to negotiate any greater jumps than 35-45 miles and that it is necessary, therefore, to send the same birds week after week, never missing 'the weekly step up' in distance. Nothing could be further from the truth.

Pigeons that are raced week after week, through a gradually increasing schedule of distances on the Natural System, soon get stale and bored. If you watch the performances of these week-by-week pigeons you will see them slow down while the birds will lose their fire and dash. This is no way to race pigeons successfully.

By the time the yearlings take over from the two-year-olds the programme will be reaching the 150/200-mile stage. If in the mean time the yearlings have been trained up to 100 miles they may be 'jumped' with confidence into the races and then be stopped to allow the older birds to be 'jumped' in for the distance events.

Beginners must not be afraid to 'jump' pigeons, in fact, better results will be obtained from two-year-olds and upwards if they are jumped into the long races. They should give much better results than birds whose energy has been ground down week after week in monotonous racing. I have jumped pigeons from 50/100 miles into races of 450/550 miles with favourable results. Remember that as youngsters and yearlings the two-year-olds gained plenty of experience along the road which they are now negotiating for the third season running. They know how to fly with the 'drag' and if you have managed them in accordance with the instructions given in the appropriate chapters of this book they should be extremely fit and ready to go. It is as well for you to remember that the race is won by the fittest pigeon, who is also the fastest over the course, so that stamina as well as physical well being must be taken into account.

Pigeons cannot and will not race well if they are not well trained before the season opens and if the good training is not continued in between the races.

No beginner should be satisfied with racing his pigeons to 300 or 400 miles. The reason why so few club members turn up with birds at the marking station for 400/600-mile races is because they wear out their birds in the week-by-week racing. The ambition of every beginner must be to fly the longer distances. One good performance in a classic race is worth all the piffling little club performances at short and middle distances achieved in a lifetime. The farther the distance at which the bird put up its performance the greater the honour bestowed on the fancier in his fellow fanciers' eyes.

Too many novices imagine that because they were unable to afford to buy expensive stock their birds will not have 'the class' to compete against the teams of more wealthier fanciers. This need not be the case. Obviously, one needs to start with well-bred birds but I advise novices not to spend large sums of money on acquiring champions. Look patiently round and find a loft which contains good stock and from which birds can be obtained at reasonable prices. If the owner demands high prices look elsewhere.

Pigeons have been purchased at prices well in excess of £1,000 each but although I have paid high prices for birds I can confirm that I have bred birds of equal merit from stock costing around £30 each. Price is no criterion of success. Exceptionally good fanciers will get better results when racing mediocre stock than the merest novice can hope to rival if working with the bluest of blue-blooded pigeons. Management and training, the twin skills of pigeon racing, is probably the most important combined factor and definitely more important than the aristocracy of the blood.

Many successful fanciers tend to cultivate two separate and distinct strains in their lofts. Because genuine long distance strains are not likely to cut any ice in the short and middle distance events an experienced fancier may keep his old tried and tested long distance team but has something nippier for the early races. This is a point well worth remembering. The late Vic Robinson once complained about his lack of success in races that fell short of Nantes while beyond Nantes he was one of the greatest flyers of all time. He built a special loft for short distance racing but staffed it with birds from his long distance family so his attempt was doomed from the outset.

The results of pigeon races are influenced by the weather ruling at the time. Note that the average weight of a racing pigeon of good strain is about 16 ounces. Hens run slightly less than this weight. The result is that the pigeon goes where the wind listeth. If the race is being flown from North to South, then a beam wind from the East will force birds to fly a course which tends more and more (according to the distance) to veer to the West. This means that fanciers whose lofts are situated in the East of the line-of flight are going to be unlucky.

Teaching birds to fly a certain course is one thing. Man proposes but on the day of the race the wind disposes and it is not respecter of persons, or pigeons.

The worst wind (apart from that coming from the East) is the head-wind. If it blows with any force at all the result of the race is predictable – a smash! This terminology is indicative of a disaster in which many, many birds will be lost and those who manage to return home will have survived a considerable ordeal, and lost much body weight.

No fanciers should blame convoyers who are not, and never have been, ruthless butchers of racing pigeons. Yet, after every race, in which losses have been abnormal, many fanciers demand the head of the convoyer, preferably on a plate. If the average fancier knew as much about the weather as any convoyer he would know that the last man to blame is the convoyer. The first is the fancier himself for not getting his birds fit enough to fly against adverse weather. No censure and no condemnation can be too strong for him. Next is invariably the weather. In long distance racing the weather can be fond and fair at the start, deteriorate half way along the route and become impossible in the home area.

I once drove a car from Scotland to the South of England. I started in drenching rain which stayed with me until I reached Yorkshire which was sweltering in a heat wave. About 150 miles from home I ran again into pouring rain which stayed with me even when I was garaging my car. It is possible that fanciers in Yorkshire that weekend would have wondered why the pigeons had not been tossed in Scotland, or in the South of England, so beautiful were the weather conditions in which they sun-bathed.

There are certain weather conditions which though favourable to look at spell disaster to the racing pigeons. Some refer to this kind of weather as 'atmospheric' and hint darkly at mystery conditions which no one has yet understood, or solved. In point of fact it occurs only when there is east in the wind. The sun shines, the skies look blue and the wind is not much more than a cooling zephyr but so far as pigeons are concerned destruction stalks abroad. Experienced fanciers know the signs and they also know what to do. If they have birds away in race panniers they pray. If at home they double-lock the loft door. The really experienced fanciers can smell this menacing weather that is sent by the sirens of hell. Unfortunately, a number of convoyers who are otherwise weather-trained cannot smell it and now and again they fall for it. It only happens in June and August, never in any other month, as our racing calendar kept over the years will bear witness. In June it falls between the 7th and 14th day, in August it occurs only at the beginning of the month.

Most British fanciers fly to the nest but on the continent the favourite method is the Widowhood System which is alleged to have been invented by Hansenne. This system is immediately opposite to the Natural System and must be regarded as somewhat artificial. I refer to it as 'artificial' only because it requires both cock and hen to live a life which is far from natural.

I have no space in this book in which to delve into the system as I would like so I must deal with it briefly. In effect, after raising a first round, usually a single-reared squeaker, the parent birds are allowed to nest again and sit the eggs for ten days after which the hen is taken away. There are variations on this method but I can only sketch in the system in broad outline herein. The hen is taken away to a loft and aviary, the latter being a must. There she sits in the aviary all day long (it is necessary to keep them out of the loft in daylight hours or hens would mate and sit eggs) while the cocks only inhabit the racing loft.

It is at this stage that the fancier must use his loaf. On the one hand he must stop his hens from mating with each other and on the other he must stop his cocks from fighting. If you force celibacy on your cocks you must expect to suffer troubles similar to those that would occur if you confined a number of men in a room and gave them nothing to do and no enforced discipline to restrain them. The Stress Syndrome would take over and there would be fights galore.

What is almost as bad as the fighting is the cocks' sudden loss of appetite. I have seen the extent to which some fanciers have gone to tempt their widowhood cocks to eat an adequate ration of food. Obviously, if they eat too little they will lose strength and become emaciated, unfit to race.

I have read books on widowhood racing in which the authors advise fanciers to show the hens to the cocks on day of marking for a race but the continental experts with whom I have discussed this system of racing advise against it. They point out that the showing of the hen to the cock (such as by locking her in a compartment of the nestbox, so that the cock can see her but not get at her) greatly excites the cock and spoils his chances of winning.

There is another theory about Widowhood racing which I have never seen performed, practically in any widowhood system loft. 'You need,' they say, 'the kind of hen which is exceptionally affectionate so that the moment her cock returns from a race to find her in his nestbox she gets to work caressing him and making him feel that it is a very good thing to dash home at top speed to find the little woman at home."

I cannot remember how many times I have sat in a widowhood loft and seen the cocks come home. They all behaved in the same way, in any loft. First they went to the drinker and enjoyed a long pull. Then they picked up a few grains and then moments, and sometimes even minutes, later, they flew up to their nestbox, entered it, and then settled down for forty winks. I never saw one hen so much as blink when the cock walked into the box. Mostly the hen sat in silence beside the cock, quite content to stand there while the old chap rested. Later on there would be some petting but the moment the fancier saw them at it he would remove the hen and take her away.

I do not wish to deprecate the widowhood system which has its many good points but I must say I've never seen more misery than in the hens' aviary where they sit, day in and day out, the picture of a miserable animal. Further, I can't believe that the hens will not deteriorate in such conditions. Most continental fanciers allow their racers to rear a late nest (usually in September) as a 'consolation' for the whole summer of celibacy.

I should advise new starters that not all cocks will race well under the Widowhood system. Some go off and try and find a female whom they can bring home. On the other hand, cocks who will work to the system put up some very fast times indeed. It is also said that widowhood cocks do not excel in long races but this is not my experience.

The first British fancier to achieve fame as a Widowhood flyer was my old friend, Fred Shaw, of Denton, who at the end of the first world war imported some expensive pigeons from Renier Gurnay of Vervier, Belgium. According to Fred Shaw, Gurnay was Hansenne's 'boy' and learnt the system from that great master. Fred built himself a loft to the design drawn by Gurnay which I have seen and studied. It was an 'open door' loft and the first of its kind in this country. I always insisted that Fred's 'open door' was one of the main reasons why for six years he was almost unbeatable. He gave the Lancashire sport such a skinning that big and prosperous clubs folded up when he flew in them. Some disbanded and re-formed to get him out and isolate him. His Gurnays flew, and homed, like bullets out of a gun and those fanciers who were sent to spy on him claimed they had never seen anything like it before.

However, fanciers flying the Natural System intelligently also produce birds that fly like bullets out of guns so in my opinion there is little to choose between the systems except that the widowhood system is less demanding on one's time and labour.

I have already mentioned that in Natural Racing one can fly both the cock and the hen. No new starter should believe, even for one moment, that the cock is superior to the hen as a racer. According to the records, in long distance classic racing the hen has the edge on the cock. However, because of their tendency to get themselves in egg, hens are more difficult to race than cocks, in fact, they cannot be raced with such frequency so they often have to be 'jumped' into an event. This fact reinforced what I have already written on the subject, viz. that a 'jumped' pigeon usually gives better results than one raced regularly.

I can still remember the time when I was left with fifteen odd hens due to an accident. I kept them in an aviary until marking day when I then let them into the loft where I kept three odd cocks. The capers of those hens was too funny to watch. Their performance in the races was much more profitable than the work done by the widowhood cocks. Australian fanciers in one State tell me they race both cocks and hens when separated (never to the nest) and get excellent results but the above incident of the odd hens is my only experience of racing unmated hens.

Racing old birds successfully is largely a matter of observation and study. One needs to watch the training closely, looking for the consistent pigeons and if flying on the Natural System the nest condition is also important. The fancier who knows his birds well, their characters, likes and dislikes, is likely to do very much better than he who doesn't trouble to distinguish one bird from another.

Many writers have written millions of words about the kind of care that should be given to pigeons after they have homed from a race. Most of them advocate stopping the bird from getting at its normal diet and feeding it only on small seeds. What they fail to realise is that the oil seeds are harder to digest and that it is inadvisable, at all times, to interfere with a bird's normal diet. It gets used to what it is given and wants nothing else. It would certainly resent any attempt to deprive it of its normal diet at the normal time.

Pigeons that home from a race aren't ill and they don't need any pampering. They may be tired, in which case they need rest, and they may be hungry, so they must be given food, the kind they are used to. I make only one change in the loft on race days. I wait until I have calculated the approximate time the bird is due to home and then I change the drinking water, replacing it with warm water in which I have poured a little syrup. I can't believe that ice-cold tap water is the best thirst-quencher for a pigeon who has worked hard over many, many miles.

X

The Drag

Since time immemorial pigeon fanciers have referred to a flock of racing pigeons homing from a race or training toss as 'a drag'. Even so, all drags are not the same, in origin, in number or in quality.

Trace the British sport to its grass roots and you arrive at its nursery, so to speak, which is the local pigeon club (or homing society) which is directly affiliated to its Union. Therefore, the pigeon fancier contends primarily for the honours his local club can bestow. However, apart from being a member of a 'union' which is the central governing administrative body of the sport, the club is also economically compelled to affiliate with yet another pigeon racing organisation, the Federation.

Whereas the Union legislates and governs, the Federation of Clubs is an organisation that is created purely and simply to convoy (to transport under supervision) the race birds for members of those clubs affiliate with the Federation. The economics of this convoying federation are simple. They are based on the unarguable assumption that a large number of birds can be transported at a much cheaper price than a mere handful of racing pigeons.

When the logic of this simple Economic fact finally sank into the minds of pigeon fanciers they were not prepared to leave transportation of birds at federation level. Instead, they formed supra-organisations known as Combines and Amalgamations in which Federations affiliated to produce even greater numbers of birds for transportation, still according to the hard-bitten commercial principle that the greater the numbers, the cheaper it is to handle each one of the mass.

When British Railways, in an act of self-immolation, deliberately priced pigeon traffic off its rolling stock, The Fancy made heavy capital investments in the modern Road Transporters. These specially designed and specially constructed vehicles cost upwards of £7,000 each and each carries thousands of pigeons, even as many as 6,000 per vehicle. So, racing pigeons which for a century were conveyed to race points by rail now take to the roads. Here again, economics are founded on numbers so the bigger the drag the cheaper it became, per capita, to transport and convoy the birds to the racepoints. In view of what has happened in the field of racing pigeon transport no one could accuse me, or anyone else, of pipe-dreaming when we predict that the sport one day will become an aircraft-owning fraternity, sending all its birds by air transport.

As the sport is organised at the present moment it is the responsibility of the local club (over 3,000 of them are affiliated to the Royal National Homing Union) to mark its members' pigeons (viz., ring the leg of each bird with the special rubber race ring) and basket or crate them, ready to be picked up by the convoying organisation's Road Transporter. The local club also supervises the setting and checking of pigeon timers into which members must insert the 'race rubbers' taken from the legs of their homed racing pigeons. The special design of the Road Transporter makes it possible for the convoyer (official in charge of the transporter and its race birds) to effect a simultaneous liberation of the birds. This means that the entire 'drag' can become airborne at the same time, an operation which was not possible when birds were transported by rail. After liberating the birds the convoyer must report by telephone or telegram to the Race Controller at the organisation's home end, the time of liberation and the condition of the weather as forecasted, over the line-of-flight.

Thus, with the birds now in the air, we can grapple with the imponderables that influence the homeward flight of the pigeons.

First of all, bear in mind that the mass of birds newly liberated into the air at the racepoint are really flying to a large number of lofts that are scattered about on either side of the line-of-flight but to a definite and clearly defined home area. Here note how the people who make Federation policy (delegates from affiliated clubs) defy the principles which local clubs have established to restrict their exclusive membership. The local club establishes what it calls 'a radius' of, say, three miles from its headquarters, outside of which circle no resident fancier can become a club member. A restriction of a kind is necessary, as we hope to explain later. Thus, an enveloping circle is drawn with a pair of compasses and membership is made available, by application, only to those fanciers who live within the pale.

The federation 'radius' does not work on this principle. It repudiates the simple 'radius' (circle) in preference for the 'corridor'. Therefore, the federation's restricted area is given great depth but a very limited width so that it represents a boxed zone in which its greatest dimension is along the line-of-flight and its shortest is at right-angles to the line. The choice of 'corridor' is one of two evils, with Federation delegates firmly convinced that they have chosen the right one (see Fig. 6).

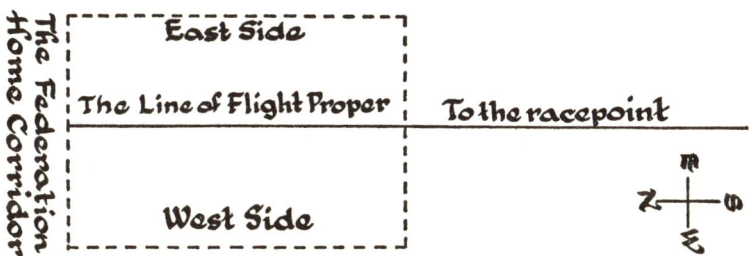

FIG. 6. *The Federation Home Corridor*

Members' lofts are dotted about in the east and west areas of the corridor as defined by the broken lines on either side of the line-of-flight

The first evil is that of the wind. It will be apparent to the beginner that regardless of whether one's birds are flying North to South, or vice versa, an East or West wind must favour those whose lofts are sited either to the left or right of the line-of-flight. Any side wind must force the birds to veer before it.

Apart from the influence of the wind there is also the effect of the 'weight' of the drag. For example, if in a drag of some four thousand pigeons three thousand were flying to the zone right of the line-of-flight, then those fanciers whose lesser number of lofts are situated on the left of the line are going to be at a disadvantage because the heavier weight of the right-homing birds must cause the drag to veer to the right of the line. So, the drag is dominated by wind and weight. By restricting the 'width' of the home corridor the Federation officials hope to reduce and minimise the influence of both imponderables.

As I said above, the 'corridor' system tends to reduce the crippling effect of 'wind' and 'drag-weight' but it ignores another evil which is inherent in the perpetual grievance which is centred in 'Overfly'. One of the first mysteries to which the beginner will be initiated is that of the 'Overfly'. By the very nature of things, some members of the club (and some members of the Federation) will have their lofts situated nearer than others to the racepoint so that the birds of one fancier will be flying a shorter distance than the birds of another. In fact, no two members will be flying identical race distances. The birds may be given the same starting line but there is no such thing in pigeon racing as a common 'finishing line'. He whose loft is sited nearer to the racepoint will necessarily fly a shorter distance than he whose loft is sited furthest from the racepoint. Such developments are the inevitable contingencies of geography. That they should become subjects for grievance is more than a pity.

The fanciers whose lofts are sited nearer to the racepoint claim they are giving valuable 'over-fly' to those members who live furthest from the racepoint while the latter retaliate by accusing the former of sharing the advantage of having 'the first drop in'. Those fanciers who are sandwiched between the 'first drop in' and the 'over-flying' members put up with all the disadvantages and enjoy none of the advantages claimed by the others.

Those who clamour against the burden of 'overfly' insist that when pigeons are flying in a drag the over-powering gregarious instinct will cause the flock to stay together and deliberately over-fly those lofts which are nearest to the racepoint and continue on, in a mass, until they reach the end of the 'corridor' of flight before the drag disintegrates so that each pigeon can 'break-away' from the mob and seek its own home loft. The disadvantage of racing birds to a loft sited nearest to the racepoint is obvious. It means that this loft's birds may be carried off, clean over the home loft, to stay with the drag perhaps for ten to twenty miles further on. Then, when the drag unsticks, birds that have overflown their home lofts must retrace their steps, so to speak, thus doubling the over-fly distance. The time lost in flying over and then flying back robs the fancier living nearer to the race-point of his true and rightful velocity and, consequently, his just reward.

The 'overfly' claim, though hotly disputed by those fanciers who are favoured by it, is no mere myth. Not one but many fanciers, finding themselves sited unfavourably on a line-of-flight, have been known to sell up their homes and move to a district which is definitely favoured by over-fly. I name no names but I personally know of a number of those who moved not once but several times until they found the ideal spot on which to erect a loft. Any member who attends a club meeting at which new applications for membership are put up for voting can sense the general opinion. Even a blind man could read the minds of the members, especially when the application is from a fancier to whom most members are required to give over-fly. In the clubs in which I have been a member I have never known such an application be accepted. Nor do I blame the members for rejecting increased risks of over-fly. Most club radii would be the better for further restriction with a view to diminishing the grievances which tend to disrupt the goodwill of so many organisations. The fairest solution to this perpetual problem is for organisations of any size to divide their competition into Sections in which corridor depths give something more like parity to competing members. No sport can thrive if it ignores the justice of equity. Arguments against overfly and the influence of the wind and drag-weight must fail. Here and there the performance of a bird will tend to disprove the claim of injustice but as in all things pigeon, the exception proves the rule.

It is also a fact that as the flying distance increases so does the penalty of overfly diminish. From very long distances (350 miles and over) overfly exerts only a minimal influence over the result. This is because the strain of the long flight nearly always leads to the destruction of the drag so that fewer and fewer birds tend to fly in company under the domination of the strong gregarious instinct of the flock. This consideration is of small consolation to club members who know that the majority of the races are flown from short or middle distances while no more than two or three events are of the long distance category.

An intact drag moves along the line-of-flight in the form of an echelon, or a huge Vee, while trailing arms stream away to the rear. If the weather and other circumstances permit the drag to stay intact until it reaches the home corridor it should in theory start to break up when it reaches the home area. One or two birds might peel off from the drag at this point but the mass will continue to fly on. I have described what might happen to a drag when it is carried along on a southerly or south westerly wind, in a northerly direction.

Where conditions are adverse (where the winds oppose the flight of the birds) the drag would disintegrate long before it reached the home corridor. What started as a great mass of pigeons speedily becomes a number of batches of birds struggling and straggling home. In these conditions over-fly exerts a much less powerful influence. You will hear fanciers say, 'This day's race will be on over-fly because the wind is on the tail of the drag.' When velocities are exceptionally low, over-fly dwindles in importance.

The imponderables I have explained above indicate that in pigeon racing the results depend not only on the bird but on circumstances beyond the bird's control. It is with this reason in mind that many pigeon journalists refer to 'the luck on the day.' The winner of a race cannot deny that in addition to owning and conditioning a very good pigeon he also has a lucky face. In my opinion the inconsistencies of weather, drag-weight and overfly, plus the gregarious instinct of the pigeon, make the sport more attractive than less and give some meaning to the saying that 'every dog has his day.'

There is nothing more harrowing or more tragic than what we call a 'smash' race. This means a race in which most of the drag is lost. Pigeon racing convoyers (sometimes also referred to as Liberators) are among the most weather-knowledgable men in the world. If experience of racing pigeon convoying was made a qualification for the recruitment of staff at Meteorological Bureaus the profession of weather-forecasting would be given a considerable status boost. Cross channel convoyers, for example, make many telephone calls along the line-of-flight to learn details of local weather before tossing their charges. This work is done in addition to obtaining official forecasts from the Meteorological people. Every possible precaution is taken to ensure a reasonable passage for the birds.

Unlike continental fanciers, British fanciers are at the first mercy of a maritime climate. Britain lies immediately in the path of Atlantic weather at its worst, weather which can change in the twinkling of an eye. And it usually does just that.

It is accepted in this country that the prevailing wind blows from the South West. It may do so on a day-by-day basis but this does not mean to suggest that the South West wind prevails on Saturdays! This makes North Road racing a tough proposition. I can remember taking part in one particular season of North Road racing when in only one race in both old bird and young bird programmes put together did a bird make a velocity in excess of 1000 y.p.m. This was in a young bird race which was won at 1004 y.p.m.* Yet when I turned round to fly the South Road I discovered that the prevailing wind had mysteriously changed its direction to Easterly!

The mass of North and South Road flyers have never conceded that it is folly to race pigeons in East winds or against head-winds. A convoyer who held birds over because the wind was Easting, or because it blew on the birds' beaks, would soon find himself on the carpet. Yet I have never flown in an East wind, or a head wind, which did not impose an enormous strain on the birds and quite often resulted in a serious 'smash.' Perhaps a time will come when prudence and deep concern for the birds will rule out both kinds of race liberation and put a much smaller strain on a fancier's breeding requirements.

If you turn your birds out to fly in an East wind you will speedily be reminded of their general reluctance to fly in it, even at exercise. They hate to rise above the roof of any house that acts as a windbrake and they soon yearn to be back inside the loft.

When a pigeon drops from a drag to the ground it does not necessarily stay down. If its purpose for dropping was to get food
*London North Road combine.

and water it might take off again and try and reach home. If the source of its water permits bathing the bird might stay long enough to enjoy it. In any event, its movements on the ground would be leisurely, costing time that must put it out of the prizes. If the bird dropped through exhaustion there would be no question of it taking a short rest before resuming its flight. Once down it would stay down because it could not restore its strength that day. If ever a pigeon with a rubber race ring on its leg enters your loft as a stray never frighten it off. Take it up and place it in a basket outside of the loft (a precaution against letting parasites or disease get into your loft) and attach troughs containing water and food. Let the bird rest in the basket for at least three days and restore its energy. Then toss it some distance away from the loft. Don't report it unless it shows a reluctance to fly away.

There will be those who will wish to quarrel with me when I refer to the 'pilot' birds who lead the drag. They will deny that such birds exist. Yet it is on record that any organisation which changes its racepoints at the distance experiences a 'smash' race at its first attempt.

It was suggested that a race should be flown from The Faroes once in four years. This would eliminate the possibility of establishing 'pilot' birds for the second attempt. By this token every fourth-year race from the Faroes must result in a bad smash. If the Faroe Race was flown every year (even a race from Arundel) it would be mastered as Lerwick and Pau and Palamos have been mastered.

During the Second World War no club pigeons were raced from France for six long years. In the year after the ending of the war the National Flying Club organised its first post-war National Race from Bordeaux. Over 4,000 pigeons were sent in the convoy but only thirty-two of these birds were recorded in race-time which, I believe, was a period of five days from time of liberation. This race must rank as the biggest smash ever to overtake a N.F.C. drag and the reason for it happening is obvious—no pilot birds!

Every club member convinces himself that somewhere along the line-of-flight, preferably a spot near the beginning of the 'home corridor,' there is a 'breaking-point,' a place where his birds will break-away from the drag and home with astonishing speed so

THE DRAG

that he can chalk up a big win. Having chosen this mysterious 'break-away' spot the member will deliberately train his birds to fly from it, perhaps day after day, hoping thereby to impress on his pigeons' minds that when they reach this chosen tossing point they are supposed to abandon the drag and belt home at their fastest and best. I never succeeded in finding such a 'breaking-point' nor was my failure due to want of not making a diligent search for it. I can only conclude that the drag rarely adheres to any set line-of-flight and rarely flies over the same area twice in a season.

Pigeons share an understandable fear of crossing water. If the coast at Dover was joined to that of Calais by a strip of land only fifty yards wide, cross channel birds would fly along the north coast of France until they reached this narrow strip of land and then cross over to England by flying over it. Pigeons will not fly over a wide river estuary, or across a wide bay, even if in doing so they took the shortest flying course. In every instance they will fly round the estuary or bay. I entertain considerable doubts about getting pigeons to cross the Channel unless it was being used by a mass of shipping. A moving ship is a moving island to a racing pigeon.

I was returning from Guernsey one day when pigeons were liberated in a race back to England. Most of the birds in that small drag stayed with the ship on which I was a passenger until it was a few miles off Portland Bill when they, and the sea-gulls who were flying with them, suddenly cleared off in the direction of Swanage. That was one drag that was taking no chance of finishing in a watery grave. All line-of-flights plotted by organisations across channel should take into consideration the shipping lines and arrange for the birds to fly along them, in the interests of staging better channel racing.

As I have said elsewhere the only thing a fancier can do by way of insuring against big losses of birds in race 'smashes' is to train them to fly solo (by single-up tossing). Here I must record a warning. No fancier who has been racing his old birds for years on the basis of drag training (trainees always tossed in a flock) should take them out and try and make them fly single-up, unless they be no older than yearlings. His loss of old birds tossed singly would be heavy. Solo-flyers must be put to work as yearlings (youngsters if possible) and be taught to fly alone before they develop the habit of flying only in drags.

One form of racing which is actually founded on the deliberate destruction of the drag is that staged by the National Flying Club and similar organisations. In opening the races to any fancier residing in the country the N.F.C. ensures that its drag will cohese only en route to the South Coast where it must certainly break up as the birds pull away on their various lines of flight to their home areas. This National drag can arrive at almost any point along a 250-mile coastline. It has been known to hit the Cornish-coast and as far east as the coast of Kent. Normally, it will fly in over Lyme Bay and over Paignton in Devon, if there is much east in the wind. If the South West winds prevail on the day then it is likely that the birds will cross by way of the Isle-of-Wight and fly over Southampton. No one can forecast the exact spot with certainty and what I have said above is mere conjecture so every fancier is entitled to his own opinion.

Here again, bear in mind that single-up training is not to accustom the bird to flying by familiar land-marks. As I have already stated, the pigeon knows its road instinctively, so geography does not affect the issue at all. The one and only purpose of single-up training is to convince the pigeon that it has nothing to fear when flying alone. It is this fear of finding itself alone in the air that is the main cause of the 'smash' race. Those who teach pigeons when they are young that they are supposed to fly in company (and mass tossing at training stages must reinforce this attitude of mind in the bird) must not complain when outrageous weather, or some other circumstance, destroys the drag and deprives the birds of their company. The first sensation that would overcome any pigeon that found itself suddenly abandoned in the sky a long way from home, would be one of panic. It would try and roost and wait for another drag to fly over and then try and join it. This is the reason why so many pigeons lost at this week's tough race limp home with the birds that are sent to the following week's race over the line-of-flight. The lone stray waits for the drag that might bring it home and some wait for so long that out of sheer desperation they join the ranks of the street and steeple-sitters.

A racing pigeon drag is a very complex problem which deserves our serious study. Of one thing we may all be sure and that is that the main effect of a drag on the birds is to convert an instinct into a habit which so often rebounds adversely on those who promoted it in the first place. Only those fanciers who shrug off trouble in their attempt to rectify the worst aspects of the drag are entitled to beat it, and ward off its worst consequences.

XI

'The Eye-Sign'

Ever since men became pigeon fanciers they sought after a sign on a pigeon which, like the hall-mark embossed on precious metal, would indicate the true worth of the bird. This search lasted for at least a century during which time the Fancy Press often reported that someone had claimed to have discovered the secret of how to grade and value a racing pigeon (as a potential race winner, or breeder of winners) without first going through the formality and expense of engaging the bird in a race as a test of its racing abilities. In Gt. Britain, as elsewhere, wherever pigeons were raced the men who competed with them strove to uncover the common factor among winning birds.

I remember a case in the early 50's when a leading group of fanciers in Belgium was working to establish 'Wing Theory' as the key to solving the 'hall-mark' question. Every new big race-winning bird was pounced upon and examined and – Lo and behold! – its wing conformed to the new Wing Theory. That is, the Wing Theory held sway until Mons Gobert of the famous Alaska Lofts at Jumet invited the disciples of this new theory to inspect his great Mosaic Cock whose wonderful performances in classic races had earned for it the title of 'Champion of Belgium'. To their consternation the Mosaic Cock's wing did not accord to the rules of the new Wing Theory. Instead, it flouted them!

What surprises me about some fanciers (and when I use the word 'some' in this context I really mean the 'majority') is that they stubbornly refuse to accept the principle that 'the exception proves the rule.' Show them just one big-winning bird whose 'hall-mark' does not confirm to the sign previously confirmed as a common factor in several hundred other winners and they promptly repudiate the sign as not having any real significance. No doubt many a promising new lead was abandoned too soon, just because of a solitary example of non-conformity. To say that pigeon fanciers, as a rule, are mildly sceptical is to make the under-statement of the century.

I, too, spent much time in looking for this 'hall-mark' which on sight alone would indicate whether a pigeon was the exceptional bird, or just a mediocre specimen but even when I thought I had found it I lacked the means for subjecting it to anything like a real, scientific test. That is, until 1945 when, with a number of other fanciers, I helped to found the monthly pigeon journal, *Pigeon Racing News & Gazette,* and became its first Editor, an office that passed to my son some five years ago.

The new journal had a staff and journalistic contributors in every district of Great Britain, so for the first time, I was at the head of a network of fanciers whom I might be able to enrol as willing participants in a scientific investigation into what subsequently became known as 'Eye-Sign,' in fact, I was the one who actually coined the title and used it in the first textbook that was ever written on the subject, my book 'The Secret of Eye-Sign.'

Unlike all the other searchers after truth (excepting only Gigot) I believed that the sign we sought would be found in the pigeon's eye. Gigot, who thought along similar lines about half-a-century before me, would have been 100 per cent successful if he had carried his researches further but, perhaps like me before the launching of the journal, he lacked the facilities for prosecuting his enquiries.

You may ask why I was so interested in the pigeon's eye? Well, if the size of a pigeon's eye is compared with the size of its body, it becomes an enormous organ. Its eyes are so large, and protrude into the interior of its skull so far, that the backs of the eye-balls roll on each other. The pigeon's eye is even larger than its proper brain. It has also been proven that the pigeon's visual acuity (the keenness of his eye-sight) is about eight times stronger than that of the best human eye (according to the count of the rods and cones on the retina). No intelligent pigeon fancier would

EYE-SIGN

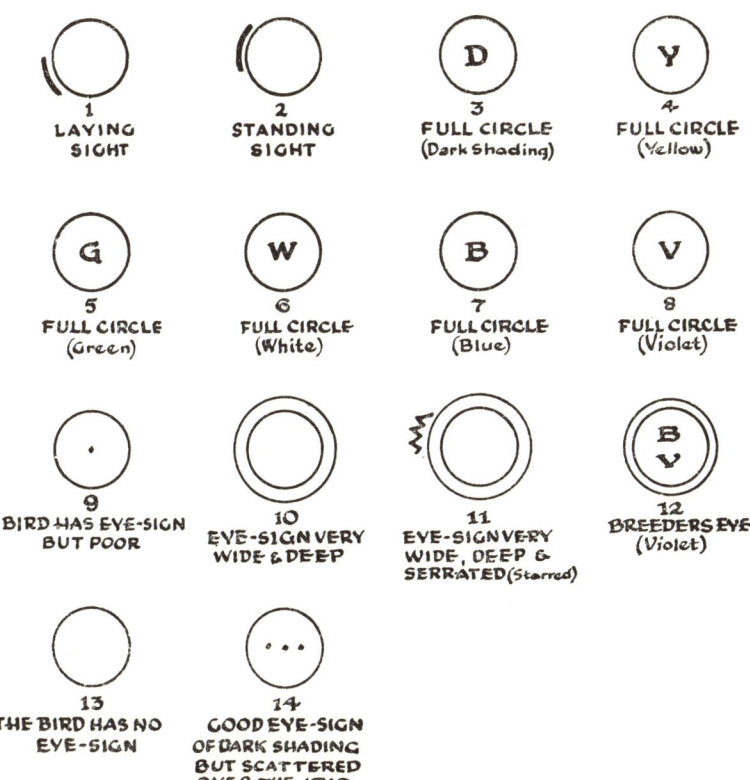

FIG. 7. *The Eye-sign Inspection Code*
The illustrations show a simple code for recording the results of eye-sign inspections

let these facts go by default without asking himself the reason why a pigeon is endowed with such superior vision. I asked myself – why is the eye and its acuity so important to a pigeon and why should its sight need to be eight-times keener than ours?

At this stage of my mental exercise on this subject it occurred to me that as Nature insisted on all members of a specie being slightly different, then I could expect to find variations in the visual acuity of pigeons, viz. that some of the pigeons would necessarily have better eye-sight than others. The thing to do was to discover what eye-factor indicated good, bad and indifferent eye-sight. I believed that if I mastered this factor I would be in a position to sort out keen-eyed birds from birds with poorer vision. That the ultimate test was to prove that the champion racers and and producers do possess the keenest eye-sight had not occurred to me at that stage of my enquiries.

Altogether the *Gazette* team carried out in excess of ten thousand separate eye inspections. My job was to collate their reports and produce them in the form of statistics. It was a hard but engrossing task and it led to the discovery of much more than we set out to learn. Later, I personally extended the eye-testing to continental lofts. Records of the number of my cross-channel eye-inspections read like this:—Fabry, Liege, 300 pigeons. Brochart, Liege 258. Van der Esp, Ostend 234, Delbar, Renee 312, Vandenbuscche, Ghent 236, Robert Sion, Mouvaix 323, Vandenbroucke, Wielsbeke 279, Nachtergaele, Zulte 128, Royal lofts of Holland, Suesduk, 216, Vanbruaene, Loew 472, Williquet Bros 501, Gobert, Jumet, 344, Swaeneopol 246, Boitselier 290, and so on. Add the numbers together and the total of eye-inspections becomes formidable. So does the sum total of the hours I have spent on the eye-inspections. As I aged, so I found that the task became more laborious. At Robert Sion's loft I was on my feet for seven hours.

To speed up the recording of the result of eye-inspections I invented a system of coding the eye-sign grading (See Fig. Three) Others who carry out the eye-sign grading in lofts, or even at exhibitions and shows, may find that my coding system will save them considerable time; it is easy to follow.

When we started our investigations into the verity of 'Eye-Sign' we were interested only in the dark shadow which rings the eyes of good pigeons. We knew that if this black circle was intact (completely surrounding the pupil) and very wide, as well as being very black, if possible with its outside edge serrated, or starred, one was inspecting a bird of high racing and breeding potential. However, before we finished our more than ten thousand eye inspections we discovered that 'Eye-Sign' also manifested itself in colours, namely, the common yellow, with its composite when black superimposed on the yellow circle, white, blue, green (which is really a dirty yellow, produced when the black super-imposes the yellow) and Violet. Whereas green is not properly a green the blue, white and violet are of that colour.

Plainly, Gigot, who carried out some work on this subject many years ago (previous century) foundered because he had not discovered that the dark shading (to which he refers in his book) was substituted by the above mentioned colours. He appears to have known absolutely nothing about the coloured Eye-Signs at all. This means that he might have rejected birds who lacked the dark shading in the eye, even rejecting and disposing of the super-value of 'violet' because it was not of the dark shading! If he did do this he was demonstrating the danger of just a little knowledge. Perhaps the important dividend paid by my investigation into 'Eye-Sign' was the revelation of the coloured signs and the enormous part they play in Eye-Sign gradings. It was when we were able to line up the coloured signs with the dark shading that the code was complete and the riddle of Eye-Sign finally solved. The 'hall-mark' we had sought so diligently had been discovered for all fanciers to share in!

When I finished collating the enormous mass of detail produced by over ten thousand eye-inspections I went to tour the lofts specially to prove to myself that my Eye-Sign Formula of Recognition was wrong. Right up to the end of the 1950's I travelled Great Britain and the continent, trying very hard in hundreds of lofts to prove that 'Eye-Sign' was nothing more than an interesting theory which was of no practical value to The Fancy. I failed to do so!

Earlier in this chapter I referred to Mons Gobert of Jumet, Belgium, whose Alaska Lofts were world famous. At the time I called on him he was the recognised Champion of Belgium. His loft was the second storey of a great barn that stood behind his house. It was the first loft I had ever visited whose floor was covered with a thick (9 inches) layer of chopped straw. The pigeons were even nesting in it so one had to be careful where one put one's feet.

Naturally, in the course of the loft visits and during her work with me, my wife had acquired a tip-top knowledge of 'Eye-Sign' and knew how to grade birds by applying the Formula of Recognition. Usually, she made the records in the book while I dictated the code readings of each bird. On this occasion she stepped ahead of me into the loft, pointing to first this and then that bird, as it stood on its perch, as having exceptional 'Eye-Sign'. After a while, Mons Gobert, who had been listening somewhat unattentively to my interpreter, whose love of the sound of his own voice was of the rapturous type, jumped and shouted something in French (he lived in the Walloon district).

'What did he say?' I asked my interpreter.

'He says he has been watching your wife and she has just pointed out the fifteen young birds who won prizes in last week's national race. He wants to know how she did it without touching the birds?'

I tried to explain, through my interpreter, how my wife had graded the Eye-Sign in the birds' eyes, awarding top points to those whose 'Eye-Sign' was the best and 'the mostest'. Gobert's face was thunderstruck. Quite plainly he had never witnessed a demonstration of this kind before our visit. He became thoughtful, bit his lip, and disappeared. Later, we heard his raised voice, calling to us to descend the stairs and meet him in the courtyard between his house and the loft.

He was standing beside a basket which contained six pigeons, all light blue chequer cocks. It seems that four of the most expert fanciers in all Belgium had called at his loft the week previous to our visit and although invited to handle the birds and select the particular cock which had won the recent San Sebastian national race for Mons Gobert, not one of them had been successful. What he wanted to know was whether I could pick it out merely by studying its eye and without handling the pigeon. I did not hesitate to say that it would be very easy for me to do so.

Of course, it was childishly simple to identify the bird. I studied the eyes of all six and knew I had found the winner when I came across a really superb 'violet'.

Gobert threw his hands up in astonishment and insisted that we should all traipse back to his house where he intended to regale us with champagne to celebrate the occasion. According to the interpreter, he said, 'Never in my long life as a fancier have I ever seen anything to equal such a great feat; it would be criminal to let it pass without a libation.'

When I pointed out that any eight-year-old child who knew about 'Eye-Sign' could have given a similar performance I was reminded of the devilish modesty of the English whose one mission in life appeared to be self-deprecation. 'Le Anglai,' said our interpreter, trying to keep up with Gobert's flow of language, 'is the same everywhere, he ridicules and abases himself, fearing to give 'imself any credit in case 'e grow zee big-'ead, eh?' While I sat in his lounge and sipped a fine champagne Gobert brought basket after basket of pigeons to me for grading, according to the Formula of Recognition.

'He can't understand it,' the interpreter mumbled into my ear, 'you have inspected over 200 pigeons and never once has your selection been wrong. He thinks you are using magic!'

There is nothing magical about the use of 'Eye-Sign'. It only appears to be the practice of magic when the selection is done before the uninformed. Let us begin the explanation by agreeing that the race is won by the fittest bird on the day. Fitness is the fruit of good health. Now, if a human being, a cat, or dog, or a pigeon starts to ail where does it first show signs of the trouble that besets it?

In its eyes! I associate good health with good eye-sight, poor health with poor eye-sight. A number of fanciers say I am wrong but not one of them has been able to prove himself to be right. On the other hand, I have grown weary of proving that the 'Eye-Sign' selection is always right. So, a bird with the best and keenest visual acuity is one who consequently has the best chance of putting up the best performance of the day. That a pigeon with very poor Eye-Sign is purblind is, as a statement, no longer debatable.

I could fill this book with reports of the innumerable occasions on which I have been challenged (or requested) to select champion pigeons at strange lofts but the space is not available. However, I will mention just two instances of successful selection and which are relevant to this chapter.

Over ten years ago I was approached by Mr Reg Christopher of Modern Hatcheries, Fontmell Magna, Nr Shaftesbury, Dorset, who asked me to supply him with a pair of birds who could breed him the winner of the N.F.C.'s Nantes National race. This was a tall order because upwards of 10,000 racing pigeons of the veritable 'cream' of British bloodstock competes in this annual classic. However, people like me, who go about the sport and claim that they have found the 'hall-mark' of the champion and can recognise it when they see it, should not shirk such issues. I matched him a pair for 'Eye-Sign' which bred him two cocks who, as yearlings, won him 1st and 2nd Nantes National. I think Reg Christopher is the only fancier to win 1st and 2nd in the same national race. Naturally, he handled the cocks with great expertise – the bird can't do it all.

Mr John Reid of 3 Rae Street, Stenhousemuir, Larbet, Scotland, is a very famous fancier who asked me to send him something special. He didn't mention that he wanted birds to breed him national winners but who would dare to send him anything that couldn't? Here again, I matched a pair by 'Eye-Sign' and sent them along. He bred two hens and a cock from this mating before returning my pair. Both hens won prizes in Scottish National racing and the cock was responsible for breeding the outright winner of a Scottish National Race.

One thing you can always rely upon in a loft where the owner is an expert selector by 'Eye-Sign' viz. he doesn't keep any rubbish. Soon after establishing the verity of 'Eye-Sign' as a 'hall-mark' I went through my entire stock and by the end of the day I was a very chastened fancier. I was elated when I went to bed that night but convinced, as never before, that no fancier, however brilliant he might be, can tell a good pigeon just by handling it. Agreed, he can tell whether the bird is useless physically but no amount of prodding with his fingers can tell him if the bird is a champion, or ever likely to breed one. Only the 'Eye-Sign,' that infallible indicator, can solve that particular problem.

It is important for the novice to understand that while the individual 'Eye-Sign' indicates the individual pigeon, even its individual potential, something more is needed when it is proposed to bring two pigeons together in a mating. This practice is called 'matching' and quite apart from balancing the two birds' physical characteristics and cast, one must also take 'Eye-Sign' grading into consideration. Some Eye-Signs match but most don't and those that don't are a sheer waste of time in the breeding loft. It must be remembered that as a sex hens selected for a career as producers, need specialised feeding from the time of hatching to assist the development of robust good health without which they are a dead loss as breeders.

Much practice is needed before any fancier should set himself up as an Eye-Sign Expert. One must study eyes of literally thousands of pigeons in many, many lofts before committing oneself to making judgements. I know 'it is all in the book' but much practice teaches one how to interpret the book in the way the author had in mind.

In this way one learns how to sift the good from the bad and indifferent types. One look at the eye and you know whether you are looking at a champion or a potential champion, or at the eye of a bird whose future is destined to be mediocre, or very bad. The next thing to learn is which 'Eye-Sign' will match to produce champions and this calls for even more skill and knowledge of the subject. Yet the work and worry of acquiring skill at Eye-Sign recognition is well worth the effort that must be made.

Plenty of fanciers have adversely criticised and disparaged my work on behalf of 'Eye-Sign' but that is in the very nature of things. I am regularly attacked in the Fancy Press, usually by pigeon dealers and auctioneers but I can't say that I mind. If I did I would have been stung to retaliate but I never do. The pigeon dealers and auctioneers, who are the chief opponents of 'Eye-Sign' attack it because they wish to sell all the birds they are offering to fanciers, not just those birds which are worth buying. The chief buyers of pigeons are not the experienced, informed fanciers, who in most cases acquire 'crosses' by exchanging youngsters with other leading fanciers but the novice and the last thing the dealer wants to see is a new starter inspecting the eyes of his wares through a magnifying glass.

The mechanism of a pigeon's eye is complex, beautiful and in the nature of a miracle. The pupil in the centre of the iris is a transparent membrane which is manipulated by Ciliary and Radial eye-muscles which contract the diameter of the pupil or cause it to dilate. The former action reduces the amount of the reflected light that is allowed to enter the eye, the latter increases it. The pupil thus controls the amount of reflected light that is allowed to enter the eye and flood onto the Rods and Cones on the light sensitive surface of the Retina.

The Retina is the back wall of the eye and its surface is extremely light-sensitive. It deflects light reflections and interprets them when they fall on the Rods and Cones. The Rods react to low light intensities (poor light) and they record in monochrome (black and white). The Cones handle the high light intensities which are, of course, reflected colour. The vast number of Cones on the pigeon's Retina confirms the bird's ability to see colour.

On dark, moonless nights only the Rods are powerful enough to pick up poor light and this is the reason why nocturnal vision is restricted to monochrome (black and white) pictures.

Unlike our eyes, the Cones on a pigeon's Retina contain what is known as 'Oil Droplets.' These 'droplets' are normally coloured Red, Yellow and Orange. The scientists have established these 'oil droplets' as light filters. Thus, the droplets filter out colours in the upper end of the Spectrum (those in Ultra-Violet) and no doubt they effectively diminish, if they do not entirely exclude, the sky's blue glare. This is an important function because it is possible that the bird's Retina, which is eight-times more light sensitive than ours, might suffer damage from high thermals built up by sky glare. On the other hand, we are bound to speculate on the possibilities of the 'oil droplets' enhancing the bird's vision at the opposite end of the Spectrum, the Infra-Red. This may account for the reason why so many pigeons have homed successfully through mist and fog and in conditions of abominably poor light.

For some time we toyed with the notion that 'Eye-Sign' was produced by a pigment in the iris but in recent years we have leaned towards the theory that 'Eye-Sign' is really a shadow reflected in the pupil (the Crystalline Lens). This theory is supported by the fact that the moment a pigeon dies its 'Eye-Sign' completely disappears. Whatever it is that causes 'Eye-Sign' to appear in the bird's iris we know that it can be seen, assessed and graded by those who are competent to classify it, according to my original and still valid Formula of Recognition.

The early antagonism of over 25 years ago, as demonstrated by those who greeted the advent of my Eye-Sign revelations with a snarl instead of a cheer, has largely vanished. Ignorance must always bow to enlightenment. For some years now, show organisers have included Eye-Sign Classes in their exhibitions. My own position as a lone voice calling in the wilderness has also eased. Instead of being the sole target for ridicule and abuse I am now surrounded by 'Eye-Sign' Experts who have relieved me of the onus of ploughing a lonely furrow. Their teachings, too, propagate the new learning. That in the course of passing time I was proved to be right is of no importance and it gives me less satisfaction than I thought was my due.

The value of Eye-Sign grading and selection, in sorting out the potential of both racers and breeders, is in the new power it vests in fanciers by enabling them to select the 'best birds' on the spot, merely by using a magnifying glass. As I have never ceased to point out, the cost of a magnifying glass is trivial when compared with the enormous cost of using a basket as a means for sorting the wheat from the chaff.

In order to clarify and explain the 'Eye-Sign' I had to write a book on the subject, *The Secret of Eye-Sign*. Obviously, I cannot condense the contents of a volume into the restricted space of a chapter. Those who wish to carry their studies on and beyond this chapter are referred to the above mentioned book and its many illustrations.

XII

The Moult

All animals – including Homo Sapiens – moult every year in the process of renewing the complete outer-skin and, where applicable, fur and feather.

The moult of man can be seen when people with dry skins (it is not so easily seen on people who have what is known as a 'greasy skin') shed white powdery bits of skin, otherwise referred to as 'dandruff'. People who shed dandruff seem to dislike the process but the abundant appearance of the white powder from their skin confirms that they are in excellent health. If the dandruff condition disappeared it would be because they were ill. When a pigeon moults it sheds feathers, too, in addition to the bits of skin from its epidermis, otherwise known to fanciers as 'bloom'.

Not one but the majority of pigeon racing journalists when writing on the subject of the moult refer to the process as one which gets rid of worn, torn, stained and useless fur, or feather, purely so that the worn-out items can be replaced with brand new and therefore more desirable new body covering. This isn't true. In fact, it is a myth! Pick up the primary flights discarded by any of your birds and what do you see? That the feather it has dropped is perfect in every way. Yet the bird has moulted it out! I've never seen a moulted feather in my loft that was not the equal of any new one grown by the birds. It is so easy for a writer to jump to conclusions and by publishing them perpetuate errors which mislead those who read them.

All animals possess two layers of skin. There is the Outer which is known as the Epidermis and the under-layer which we call the

Dermis. Below the Dermis is another marginal layer whose function is to produce, in this instance, new cells. The remarkable thing about this cell-making layer, called the Germinal Layer, is the speed with which it continues to manufacture new cells for skin and feather replacement.

High-speed cell manufacture is important because a new cell thrives for only a short time after which it goes through a process of protein deposition known as 'keratinization' (just another word for 'drying-up'). The process of cell-manufacture never stops, day and night, so that on the whole it tends to make too many rather than too little new cells.

These new cells have a protein double-action, or duo-development. They 'keratinize' and form dead layers of skin from the cells which are shed from the Epidermis (outer layer of skin) as 'moult' (dandruff of the human being) 'bloom' on the skin of a racing pigeon. On the pigeon they do something else, too, they keratinize but they also sprout new feather. Some other products of these cells are claws and beaks, etc.

The animal's protective double-skin layer is a very remarkable natural product. If you think about it you will realise that it is the only protection that is afforded to an animal between itself and the hazards of the outside world. It is waterproof so that it resists water-penetration at any time. It rejects water with greater ease than the best silicones. It can put up with a great deal of friction, and being to a certain extent self-lubricating and self-cooled and apart from being highly resistant to infection by germ, bacteria and virus it is the body's only real screen against millions of types of infection.

Some animals grow hair and some feather and in each case the process is similar. If you closely examine the texture of the skin you will find that it is freely cratered and the tiny little 'crater' holes are known as 'follicles'. Some animals sprout hair from their follicles, some feather. We know that nature evolved hair before feather because the baby nestling is entirely covered with hair and no feathers; these sprout later. The hair grown by the nestling is called 'down' and is yellow in colour. It is the area of skin that exists between the follicles that moults and flakes. The process never ends throughout the year.

THE MOULT

Here I must pause to stress an important phenomenon of the moult. When a pigeon is moulting freely it is in good health. When it stops moulting it is ailing and needs immediate attention. Secondly, when the moult stops it is also because the bird is not eating its regular meals. Lack of food instantly halts the manufacturing process of the Dermis Germinal Layer. It is this cessation of the moult which causes the appearance of the 'fret-mark' on the feather's quill. This 'fret-mark' appears in the form of a slight 'crease' or indent across the central quill. It occurred when the bird stopped eating at a time when the feather was growing. Fret-marks cannot appear on the quills of fully grown feather, only on that which is in the process of growing. The absence of food quickly interferes with the intake of protein so that it is not supplied to the Germinal Layer. Result – because the feather stopped growing it also 'keratinized' – dried-up. After it had hardened the bird's regular meals were restored so it again started to re-grow the halted flight. However, it could start to grow again but it could not rid itself of the tell-tale 'fret-mark'. The position of the mark on the quill when compared with the calendar of the moult tells the exact week when the bird went without its regular meals. It takes only a day or two of starvation to cause this fret-mark to appear.

The four kinds of feather on a pigeon all pass through the process of moulting. The down feathers never stop falling. The long outer feathers of the wing (the Primary Flights) fall at intervals between the first week of June and November (if birds are mated in the spring). The Secondary Flights fall erratically and in no fixed order. The tail feathers (rectrices) fall in pairs. The feathers whose function is to cover and protect the roots of the flights and rectrices are known as Coverts and they fall during the 'Big Moult' which begins in July.

When the youngsters from its first round of eggs leave the nest the parent birds proceed to drop a primary flight. This is always the No. 1 Primary which grows next to the last Secondary flight. It is worth remembering that a pigeon standing over youngsters in the nest will not moult a primary flight, that is, until the youngsters are weaned away. So, if you wish to make any bird retain its flight, see that it has a nestling to feed.

It is when the time arrives for the fourth flight to fall that pigeons start what is known as 'The Big Moult'. This occurs roughly in mid-July when the bird is speedily divested of feather and displays large patches of bare skin. Many novices have been known to quake when beholding their birds in this rag-bag condition. Some even fear that their birds have contracted feather-rot! The last primary is not replaced until October or November by which time the plumage should be beautiful to behold. Secondaries may not all moult out in the current year.

When a pigeon is breeding it needs to be given all the nourishing food it needs so the diet must contain a high percentage of protein. Growing squeakers must also be given high protein food, scientifically balanced with vitamins and minerals. When the bird is moulting its needs are similar, it must be fed on a high protein type of diet. To keep a pigeon 'on the tooth' when it is moulting is an act of sheer folly. A pigeon who does not enjoy a good moult this year is a non-winner next year. Note that in the wild state a pigeon would eat every two hours. The moulting pigeons need access to a hopper, one always kept fully charged with food in which the Legumes pay the principal role.

If the sexes are separated when the 'Big Moult' comes on they should tend to moult faster than birds left on the nest, or together.

How does one speed up a moult? One could wish this to happen when needing a bird to 'clean up' completely in time for the exhibitions. According to what I have read (but never practised) the bird should be fed on desiccated thyroid (2/3 grams) in capsule form, taken through the mouth.

Old birds should not be raced after the third primary flight has grown. Young birds are raced even though moulting, so long as they are not bare behind the nose, on the neck and chest, and have no covert feathers missing. They may not be raced when they have a great gap in the tail. Any youngster who suffers a 'good hiding' in a hard race, when it is moulting, is going to develop nasty 'fret-marks'. It may even suffer a discoloration of the plumage in both wing and tail. As I have already pointed out, the evil of the fret-mark is in its weakening effect of the feather quill. If the quill should snap it will break at the fretted portion of the quill.

It is advisable for you to store some of the dropped primary flights (try and store at least one of each) in case one of your birds damages a Primary, or breaks one. In such an event, take a moulted matching flight from stock and cut it down to the length required to replace the part that has broken off, plus ½ inch. Take a knife and pare away the webbing from the extra ½ inch of quill at its bottom end. Now dip the ½ inch of bare quill into an adhesive and push it into the vane of the broken flight (telescoping it) making sure that the webbing of the original and the repair flights match up on the same plane. When set, the repaired feather will be just as good and effective as the original flight when it was intact.

If you find your loft is liberally sprinkled with moulted 'down' feather during the winter it is a sign that the inmates are very healthy and should develop 'racing form' in the new seasor ahead. Always watch and ensure that your birds carry plenty of 'bloom' on their feather and back.

Resist the temptation to mate pigeons early in the new year. Birds mated in January will be in the 'Big Moult' at a time when they are needed for the best races. The best time to mate is the 7/9th March. One can always count upon sunshine at the end of the first week in March. These old birds, mated 7/9th March, will have dropped only two flights by the time they are engaged in the long races.

Ignore fanciers who say they like to race a bird with 'a full wing'. Any pigeon that retains a full wing through June and July is a truly sick bird whose moult has ceased. It is a completely normal and natural thing for a pigeon to moult its feathers and it matters not if the wing is full, or minus a moulted flight, its flying ability is not impaired.

Birds should not be asked to fly and exercise when they are in a heavy moult. What they need most at such times is a quiet and unharassed life with plenty of nourishing food and baths. If they put on a little extra weight to carry through the winter months ahead, don't worry about it. They will lose the extra weight soon enough when the cock starts to chase his hen next breeding season!

XIII

Ailments and Diseases

Like all other animals racing pigeons are heirs to a wide range of ailments and diseases and each and every one of these complaints can kill the birds. Some of these diseases are rare and need never occur to bother the beginner who designs and builds a well-ventilated loft and keeps it in a high state of hygiene and who scrubs out his drinkers every day in the winter and three times a day in the summer months. Just topping up water in drinkers is not good enough. The drinkers must be scrubbed clean before being re-charged with clean tap water. Don't use an old watering can for the purpose because filth collects in the narrow spout and contaminates the water. Much better to fetch the water in a clean plastic pail.

Unfortunately, there are a number of common complaints which attack the best managed and most hygienic of lofts and it is against these scourges that the beginner must be most wary and vigilant.

The worst disease to attack racing pigeons – I deem it to be the worst because there is no medicinal cure for it – but one which can be easily prevented, is Respiratory Disease. If the beginner builds the kind of loft described in Chapter One of this book he should never be worried by a single case of it. I know that this disease is infectious, even highly infectious, but birds kept in the kind of loft I have described (known as an 'open loft') build up a remarkable resistance against infection. It was over forty-years ago that I opened up my loft and although I am quite sure my birds have been in contact with birds in race panniers who had contracted the disease not one returned to my loft as a sufferer. The common complaints that can hit any loft are as follows :—

COCCIDIOSIS

This disease is caused by an internal parasite known as the Cocci-worm which is invisible to the naked eye. This miserable, loathsome parasite is picked up by a pigeon when it is pecking around. It works its way through the bird's digestory tract until it reaches the Small Intestine. There it lives by eating away the tiny, hairlike suckers which grow from the inside wall of the Intestine and whose purpose is to suck the proteins from the digested food and pass them straight into the blood-stream. Obviously, if the Cocci-worm is permitted to stay in the Intestine and destroy the food suckers less and less nutrients will pass into the body so that eventually the bird will die from starvation. The thing to do is to get rid of the parasite with all speed and before it inflicts irreparable damage on the bird. The fancier should always keep Anti-Coccidiosis specifics by him so the bird can be dosed quickly because the Cocci-worm can kill a pigeon in 3/4 days.

It is unfortunate that when this parasite gets into a pigeon loft it breeds a colony which promptly takes up what it hopes will become permanent residence. Invariably it is attracted to the floor as being the ideal place to dig in and propagate its specie. If the floor is porous, in goes the Cocci-worm and the only way in which you can hope to get it out is by charring the entire floor surface with a blow torch. I have advised putting down a non-porous floor with a water-proof surface.

The symptoms of Coccidiosis are increasing loss of weight ('going light') greenish coloured droppings, perhaps some vomiting of corn and possibly a tendency to drink water to excess. Throughout the stages of the disease, up to the terminal one the bird will preserve a snow-white wattle, tight feather and clear eyes. Any beginner who finds a bird 'going light' but cannot detect any of the above symptoms should nevertheless pop a Coccidiosis pill into his bird's throat, purely as a precautionary measure. If the trouble is Cocci the bird should be bright and have arrested its loss of weight by next day.

AILMENTS AND DISEASES 153

There are no evil after or side effects to Coccidiosis if the bird is treated in the early stages of the disease.

ESCHERIA COLI

Otherwise known as Bacterial infection, this disease is non-infectious but it can be a killer. It occurs when the residual bacteria in the Large Intestine (where it assists with the digestion of the food) gets into a state of imbalance. It has been found that in the majority of cases this disease is the accompaniment of Respiratory Disease. The respiratory trouble lowers the bird's resistance to infection and Escheria Coli develops.

The first symptom is 'going light', diarrhoea, greenish droppings, feathers blown and then the appearance of tiny yellow pimples in the throat. The bird tends to huddle where it sits. It blows its feather because it develops a high temperature and wants air to get at its skin to cool it. It should be dosed with the proper specific immediately.

If the bird recovers from this killer complaint the yellow pimples will have disappeared to leave white spots behind in their place. These white spots are really the calcined remains of the white corpuscles of the bird's blood which died in the fight with the alien germ that caused the infection. They cannot be removed but should go missing in time.

POLYNEURITIS

This disease is caused by a vitaminic deficiency in the bird's daily diet. It is non-infectious. Polyneuritis is rife in the lofts where the diet is restricted to grain alone. I have known cases where although birds could get at an unlimited supply of mixed grain they still starved to death, for want of vitamins and minerals.

The first symptom of Polyneuritis is 'going light' and the loss of flesh is progressive but slower than in the case of Coccidiosis and Escheria Coli. The droppings become loose, greenish, watery, the bird sits huddled up while its plumage gradually loosens. The eye dulls and the nictitating membrane crawls slowly across the eye. Feathers 'blow' on nose and neck. Either the leg or the wing develops a noticeable weakness. As the disease progresses the bird will tend to sit back on its tail, throw its head rearwards to lie on its back, while its beak gapes. In some cases the suffering bird will fall over backwards.

The obvious remedy is to give the bird the vitamins and minerals whose deficiency is killing it. These include 'A' 'D' and 'B' range, especially Riboflavin, Nicotinic Acid and B.12. Alternatively, and better still, give it 'boost'. Here again, there are no after or side effects, and when cured the bird can be as good as new. The disease is not infectious.

ONE-EYED COLD

This occurs when one eye starts to water (not both) and when the water laying in the lower lid of the eye is seen to carry a number of tiny bubbles. If no bubbles are present the bird is not suffering from One Eyed Cold but from injury, probably inflicted in a fight.

Once thought to be caused by a draught, One Eyed Cold has since been proved to be a vitaminic deficiency complaint, similar to Polyneuritis but in this case the important vitamin is 'A' & 'D'. By adding this vitamin to the diet one brings about a restoration of the bird's health with no after or side effects.

CANKER (Trichmonais)

This is a common but nasty disease which is infectious but also hereditary. I eradicated this disease from my family a long time ago by disposing of every bird who contracted the complaint. While I was about it I also disposed of the parents of the sufferer. Canker shows up mainly in squeakers but although the parents never showed themselves to be cankerous I knew that they had passed the disease to their nestlings.

The symptoms are cheesy, yellow pus deposits in the mouth and/or throat. This pus must not be confused with the yellow pimples of Escheria Coli. The disease is caused by the Trichmonais germ. If the bird is not treated with the proper specific (2 Amino 5 Nitrathiazole) the canker pus will build up in its respiratory tract and choke it to death.

PIGEON POX

This disease is really the highly contagious epithelioma, Diptheria, which has its origin in filth. Racing pigeons become infected if they come into contact with street-pigeons. Pigeon Pox is similar to Chicken Pox. It begins with eruptions on the skin round the eyes in the form of greyish coloured blisters which vary in size from tiny to one as large as a Tic Bean. These blisters then develop crusty nodules and yellow spots and patches develop in the bird's throat. The only treatment for this complaint is vaccination, preferably by your local veterinary surgeon.

PARASITES

The moment you put pigeons in your loft the huge armies of parasites will try and start to move in. They attack the bird internally and externally. The worst are the Mites.

Red Mites are really grey. They do not become red until they have sucked blood from their victim. It is a third of the size of a pinhead and is fitted with four pairs of legs. It invades the loft and attacks the birds in the form of an army of many thousands. No sitting bird can stay on a nest when attacked by Red Mite. This is the cause of so many 'chilled' eggs found in deserted nests in the morning because the Red Mite usually attacks at night.

The Plumage Mite can be seen on a parasited bird if the spanned wing is held up between the eyes and a strong light source. The Plumage Mite can be seen in the form of a dirty yellow stain on the webbing on either side of the quill. This mite hangs its eggs in rows on the barbecules of the webbing.

The Depluming Mite actually burrows into the skin where it has bared a patch of its feather. If the bare patch is examined through a magnifier the remains of the feather are seen standing like tiny stumps.

None of the above mites can be disposed of by insecticides because they are not insects. One must use a proper Mite Deterrent and an ointment for the Depluming mite.

The most offending of the insects is the Louse and here again the beginner will have to contend with several species. The large one is called The Biting Louse because it bites a row of holes in the feather webbing, commonly called 'Pin-Holes'. Remember, you wouldn't be able to work properly, either, if parasites kept you awake all night!

If Red Mite attack a tiny nestling they can drain its body of blood over night. Many a fancier has gone to a loft in the morning and found newly hatched nestlings cold and dead in the nest. No doubt he imagined that the parents abandoned the nestlings but they never do this sort of thing without a very good reason. In 99 out of 100 cases they are driven off the nests by parasites.

Don't waste time painting loft walls with creosote. It gives a dark and murky interior to the loft and never keeps insects and mite out for very long. The one and only way of dealing with parasites is to make them uncomfortable to begin with and then attack them constantly with specifics.

Racing pigeons insist on drinking from dirty puddles and gutters and nothing you can do will stop them from indulging in this bad habit. The result of this practice is 'Sour Crop' which, though not a disease in itself, provides the conditions in which infection begins. You can always tell when a pigeon has contracted Sour Crop. Sniff at his breath and if it stinks its crop is sour.

If you've no specific on hand for the treatment of this condition get some charcoal (or coal dust will do) and some flour. Add a little water to the flour and roll out some little discs. Tip charcoal or coal dust onto the dough and roll it up in a ball about the size of a marble. Slightly bake. Put the pigeon on a course of about one dozen pills, one each day.

There is no cure for the hen who lays chalky eggs, eggs with little or no shell, or faulty eggs. The fault is in her reproductory system and it is nearly always permanent.

Since successive governments allowed vandals to drape ugly cables over pylons erected across our beautiful countryside hundreds of birds break their legs by flying into them. If this tragedy should overtake one of your birds obtain from the chemist a short length of bandage which has been impregnated with Plaster of Paris. Set the broken leg in its correct position and wrap some cotton-wool round it. Then bind the leg with the impregnated bandage after you have moistened it. Bind firmly but not too tightly. When it dries the bandage will harden, like cement, and make an ideal splint.

Now take an old sock and cut the toe off. Pull the sock over the bird's head and body, thus imprisoning the wings. Attach a short length of tape to each side and hook it over nails, or screws, put into the sides of the nestbox. The pigeon must be suspended in the sock for ten full days. On no account must the bird be able to put his feet on the floor of the nestbox. Now place in front of the bird, in such a position that he can get at them without difficulty, three small pots, containing food, water and grit. When the bird is taken down ten or eleven days later use pliers to break up the bandage but do it gently. Remove the plaster-bandage and the cotton wool and release the bird.

Pigeons, like all animals who root in the earth, must contract round worms. No pigeon can avoid this fate so it is the lasting responsibility of the fancier to de-worm his birds regularly, as a matter of routine.

If you wish to be sure that your birds are wormy and you don't mind going to a little trouble to find out you can apply a little test once described by 'Old Hand'.

Take the pigeon dropping you wish to test and soak it in a jam-jar of water. Next morning strain the contents of the jar through a kitchen strainer into another jar. Now add a knob of Reckitt's Blue, about the size of a maple pea and stir. Although the Reckitt's Blue dyes the water, any worms in it will show up as a darker blue. If the water is heated they will thresh about in it.

Genuine pigeon round worms cannot be seen by the naked eye so if you see any worms in a pigeon dropping they will be poultry worms. These worms are very dangerous to racing pigeons. Never let your birds get near to poultry, turkeys, or any animals of any kind, or it won't be long before they will be in trouble.

It is a pigeon's nature to 'field' so provide it with a small patch of lawn in front of your loft and try and restrict it to your grass. Otherwise, birds will certainly range off and find a field to peck over where they can be shot or killed by animals.

If you have to site your loft on an allotment, where vegetables are grown, make sure your birds cannot get at the cabbage. If they so much as peck at the leaf of a cabbage which has contracted 'club-root' they will be knocked completely off form.

Please make sure that your lawn grows no clover, especially of the specie Trifolium Dubiem. This clover is of the Lotus family and a close relative of Melilotus Alba, a clover that poisons cattle. Pigeons who can get at the Dubiem, which has a tiny yellow flower, entirely lose form.

Those fanciers who give their birds greenstuff do far more harm to their birds than those fanciers who give no greenstuff at all.

On no account allow snails in the garden. The blackbirds will kill and eat the snails but leave their shells behind. The pigeons will peck at these shells and ingest the fatal Liver Fluke.

Never, never permit a wild bird into your loft, especially the sparrow and the starling. All sparrows contract roup diseases and I've never seen one whose beak was not partially eaten away by the disease. One sparrow can infect all your birds with respiratory disease. The starlings carry the Depluming (Itch) Mite. The Depluming Mite is known as Mange on dogs and Scabies on human skin.

When the beginner finishes reading this chapter he will realise that in order to be a successful fancier he must know more – and do more – than the feeding, watering and cleaning of his birds. He must fight an endless battle against parasites and disease and be able to cope with whatever trouble comes his way.

As this book bears witness, a fancier's trouble, like a woman's work, is never ending. Such are the thrills, happiness and fraternal blessings of pigeon racing that no real fancier minds tackling trouble so long as he knows how to go about it. Herein lies the value of a good, modern textbook. It tells the way in which other fanciers solved their problems and arms the beginner with the kind of advanced information his fore-fathers in the sport never knew.

XIV

The Respiratory System

A fit racing pigeon breathes, like any other animal, through its nose but from there onwards the difference between the pigeon's respiratory system and our own is as between chalk and cheese.

In the opening chapter of this work I stressed the importance of loft design which must be based almost exclusively on a good and ample system of ventilation without which one would soon be in trouble from respiratory disease. I again stress the vital importance of adequate ventilation at all times. For instance it is not a good thing to put up shutters behind the louvres in the cold months. A fit pigeon can keep its body warm in the coldest of weather in this country and it loves the wind to play upon its plumage.

It is not a good thing, either, for you to move your birds into your friend's loft while your own is being decorated. Instead, put the birds in training baskets. The baskets can be put back into the loft when you stop decorating for the day. Your birds might overcrowd your friend's loft to the detriment of both teams of birds, or his ventilation system might not be as efficient as yours.

A pigeon has lungs like all other animals but they are small, just large enough to ensure that the blood in circulation contacts the essential oxygen breathed in by the pigeon but it respirates on the air stored in its Air Sacs. This means that a pigeon could breathe and exist comfortably if it did not breathe in any air from some three to four minutes.

The Air Sacs are made up of delicate membrane and besides acting as air storage chambers they also cushion vital organs.

There are the Abdominal Air Sacs which are dorsal to the intestines and the posterior end of the lungs. There are also two Posterior Thoracic Sacs adjacent to the sides of the lungs. Two other sacs are known as the Anterior Thoracic Sacs at the undersides of the lungs. The Interclavicular Air Sac is really two Sacs that have become one, located beneath the front end of the breastbone and the clavicle. When a pigeon coos it expels air from this interclavicular Air Sac, hence the noise it makes. The pigeon does not 'blow up its crop' in the act of cooing although this might appear to be the case. An auxiliary Air Sac lies beneath the bird's shoulder while the remaining two are the Cervical Sacs at the cervical vertebrae. Nine Air Sacs altogether.

Air is also stored in the hollow Humerus Bone which I have reported before as containing no marrow with the result that if it is broken it cannot mend.

A pigeon breathes out but it does not consciously breathe in. Its breathing system is similar to that of the bellows. Exhalation is achieved by contracting the stomach after which it is allowed to fall back into place and in doing so it brings about inhalation. This means that the volume of air in each act of inhalation is measured but is the same in quantity.

When roosting on a perch the pigeon breathes at the rate of some forty inhalations per minute. When it is flying this breathing rate is stepped up to the enormous rate of four-hundred-and-twenty breaths per minute. You might well ask why this breathing rate is stepped up by ten times the normal inhalation rate. It is because whenever a pigeon raises its wing on the up stroke it breathes in and when the wings are depressed (brought down) in the power stroke of flight the bird exhales. Obviously, the racing pigeon's respiratory system is under demands to supply really enormous quantities of air when working to produce the energy it uses up when propelling itself through the air.

We now see the connection between the Respiratory System and the huge heart, both of which combine to keep the bird airborne for long flights. Incidentally, the racing pigeon has no diaphragm so it cannot contract 'the stitch' which can inflict so much pain on human beings. On the other hand, its measured intake of air ensures the provision of plenty of oxygen.

THE RESPIRATORY SYSTEM

The beginner should watch his pigeons carefully and make sure that no respiratory trouble is allowed to develop. This disease is not inherited but if parent birds are sufferers they can pass the infection to their nestlings at the time of regurgitation of the food.

Never keep birds who have succumbed with respiratory trouble. It is possible that after treatment the bird will look as good as new and deceive you into believing that it has been cured. This is not so! The bird will enjoy a good winter but the moment it is required to feed nestlings next Spring it will again become the victim of respiratory disease and certainly pass the complaint to its nestlings.

In cases where expensive stock goes down with this disease I suggest isolating it in another loft, or hutch, where they may be allowed to go to nest and lay eggs. These eggs should be removed from their nests and taken back to the proper loft to be incubated under foster-parents. Only in this way can the sufferers be prevented from passing their infection to other birds and to their offspring.

The respected writer, 'Old Hand,' once wrote that the ideal loft would be one whose four walls were made of wire-mesh covered by a roof. I, who have been known to disagree with him at times, thoroughly agree with him on this subject, always provided the interior of the loft could be kept very dry.

If you should see one of your birds standing on a perch, or elsewhere, beak open and panting, the bird is not out of breath. Racing pigeons can never be out of breath. It is sucking in air to act as a coolant because it has hotted up its body, probably through taking unaccustomed exercise. Pigeons tend to do this when too fat inside.

XV

The Hen's Reproductory System

Most fanciers find that good hens, both as racers and producers, are numerically few and far between. This is hardly surprising since the hen of a nest pair is hatched after the cock (always supposing the two eggs contain one of each sex). The cock of the nest pair, being older and stronger, manages to grab the lion's share of the regurgitated food.

The hen is, in most instances, the weaker sex and this is noticed, when the youngsters are put into training, by the loss of hens. Later, the hen assumes a greater burden when she makes calls on her reproductory system.

Notwithstanding the hen's disadvantages and her obvious extra physical burdens I must put on record that an outstanding long distance hen, or a fabulous producer hen, is going to be long remembered when most of the cocks have been forgotten. Once or twice in a lifetime a good fancier breeds an exceptional hen, either as a racer, or a producer, and she sheds glamour on the loft and gilds the owner's reputation.

The hens are not just the opposite sex to the cocks. They are opposite in so many ways. For example, a cock can become a very friendly bird but he never surrenders his independence. You can be playing with him until he spots a hen. He is off like a shot, serenading the hen and you are put completely out of his mind. Not so with a very good hen who really takes a shine to her owner. Her loyalty is more like an expression of true love. Exceptionally tame and very affectionate hens can and do kid themselves that they are mated to their fancier-owner.

I advise the beginner not to allow any of his hens to suffer from such an illusion. I can remember the time when a Blue Chequer Hen of mine refused to have anything to do with any cock in the loft. I had only to walk near the loft and she would drop to the floor and run across it in my direction, tail half-fanned, head coyly nodding, finally to squat, ready for the expected tread. There was just one thing wrong with this association of hen and master, all the eggs she laid were unfertile, and she went regularly to nest. Therefore, although the hen's attitude might be flattering, the end product was nil. A good hen was probably wasted.

Some fanciers look on their hens as egg-laying machines but they are definitely not in this category. You can always spot a hen whose laying powers have been abused. She drops her 'undercarriage' viz her stomach and vental area drop down, giving the hen the appearance of a duck when she waddles across the loft floor.

Many hens possess faulty organs of reproduction. This is evidenced by a large number of hens who lay faulty eggs. I simply do not care for the sight of a nest containing two faulty eggs. On the odd occasion when I am required to see this unwelcome sight I immediately oust the hen from the loft. This is a weakness which I never forgive.

The hen is fitted internally with two separate systems of reproduction and they are known as the Left and Right Ovaries. At some stage of the racing pigeon's evolution the hen's right ovary became atrophied so that the new life she makes issues entirely from her Left Ovary. This Ovary is connected to her left kidney by a membrane.

The surface of the Ovary is dotted with hundreds of tiny follicles each one of which ends in a tiny egg. Thus, all the eggs a hen is going to lay in her life time are numbered the moment she is hatched. This means that when the egg ripens and falls from its follicle the follicle cannot grow another egg.

Each of these microscopic follicle-eggs contains the germ of life (germ nucleus) and the tiny blob of yolk from which the new life will extract its first nourishment. However, until the hen is driven and stimulated by the cock the follicle-eggs are neutralised and incapable of further growth.

When the hen is mated and the cock begins to stimulate her two eggs will begin to grow. Only two of the many follicles will normally respond to the stimulation, of course. This egg growth will continue so long as the cock keeps chasing the hen and going through the motions of mating. Then, when the egg-germ and the yolk have grown to maximum size the time has come for the egg to be passed to a second and separate part of the reproductive system, the Oviduct.

The Oviduct is a kind of tube, some three to four inches in length. The end of the tube that is nearest to the Ovary is bell-mouthed, shaped somewhat like a funnel. Its job is to catch the egg-and-yolk when it ripens and falls away from the Ovary. The falling egg must be caught and held firmly by this funnel-shaped tube-mouth.

I hope you will bear in mind that the falling egg has to be caught in a funnel, like a ball falling into a basket, when you are tempted to train or race a hen in egg! The hen must be perfectly still at the moment the egg falls into the Oviduct, otherwise the egg could miss the funnel.

Once grasped by the Oviduct the egg passes through the tube to that section of it where a gland produces, and wraps the white of the egg (the albumen) round and round the egg-and-yolk in a twisting motion. At its next Oviduct station the egg is given two coats of membrane (skin). It is not until the egg reaches the final station in the Oviduct, the Uterus, that it is given its hard shell. The above description describes the egg-making process briefy and simply. There is, of course, more in it than I have outlined but I try hard not to be too technical and bore the reader with unnecessary terminology.

The important thing to bear in mind is that stimulation generated by strong biological emotion is essential to the egg-making processes. Fertilisation of the egg by the cock is necessary but stimulation by the cock is vital.

Questions must arise, I know, even out of the above brief and simple disclosures. For example, when a hen has been fertilised by a cock for how long will that fertilisation last in her? It is necessary for the fancier to know the answer to this problem because if he loses the cock of a pair and replaces him, will the hen stay fertilised by her previous cock, or not?

I completely disagree with those authorities who insist that the hen remains fertilised after treading for periods of up to 14/17-days. I saw that even Levi, who set himself up as an authority on pigeon lore, fell for that inaccurate forecast. Most other authors followed his lead like so many sheep.

In my opinion, fertilisation of the hen lasts only so long as it takes the spermatozoa to reach the ovary and fertilise a follicle-egg. I will go further and say that the hen then has to be re-fertilised for her second egg to mature.

Note that from the time the egg falls into the Oviduct some forty-hours must pass before the egg can be made and delivered by the hen. This means there must be a time-space of some two days less four hours between the laying of the first egg and the second. Now, if fertilisation lasts fourteen days why do so many hens lay so many second eggs which are infertile? The reason is obvious. It is because the hen insists on standing over her first egg instead of letting the cock continue to chase and tread her. If she is not trodden by the cock after laying her first egg her second egg must be an unfertile one. I am probably the only pigeon racing texbook writer who makes this claim but you can test it for yourself in your own loft. All you need do is separate a mated pair at a time when the cock has been treading. Keep them separated for a week or ten days then mate the hen to a different cock and let her go to nest with him. According to Levi and others, the egg the hen lays for her second cock was really fertilised by her first cock, some ten days or fortnight ago. What you will always find is that the egg hatched by the pair in this test is always sired by the second cock, not the first!

The beginner is strongly advised to throw away all imperfect eggs and only allow birds to incubate what I term 'perfect' eggs. Hens who are erratic layers, who are continually late in laying (taking more than eight days from day of mating) who lay abnormal eggs, should not be kept.

It is possible for a hen to lay a 'double-yoked' egg but rarely. This kind of egg is large and blunt at both ends, without the sharper end of the single-yolked egg. It is possible to hatch out two youngsters from a double-yolked egg only if the fancier helps the babies to chip the eggs. There is insufficient room for both babies to turn and chip away the two caps from the eggs. But with the fancier's help they could be hatched out.

XVI

The Mathematics of Pigeon Racing

All newcomers to the sport of pigeon racing must recognise and accept the logic of the proposition that the world is round or, to be more precise, a sphere-shaped mass which spins on its own invisible axis at one thousand miles per hour (approx :) while it traces its orbit round the sun. With this view of the universe in mind you will appreciate that when I say we must teach a pigeon 'to fly a straight-line' its real journey is made through a section of a great arc of a very big circle.

Before men devised ways and means of flying racing pigeons in competition they had to learn and process certain facts concerning both geography and time. They came up against certain imponderables which flatly defied simplification. For example, most races have a common starting and finishing line to which all competitors are subject. In pigeon racing all birds are subject to a common start-line but every member's birds must fly a different length of course and therefore finish at a different line. This also means that whereas all the birds start at one and the same moment in time they will all have different finishing times. The difference in the length of every member's course may differ by a yard or two to one of miles, depending on the length of the home 'corridor' and the geographical position of the home loft.

When tackling the above problem the pigeon racing pioneers felt the pressing need for a system for calculating each member's race distance between the racepoint (place where the mass of competing pigeons are to be liberated) and his home loft. This calculation was to be in miles and yards and it was required to be as accurate as possible.

The method of calculation chosen is known as The Great Circle System which, on Mercator's Chart, is shown as a curve and is the shortest distance between any two places on the surface of the earth. Remember, the earth is a sphere so that any journey made over its surface must pass through an arc. The measurement of members' race distances by this method calls for calculations to be made by spherical trigonometry so the work is obviously a job for professional surveyors. The Unions appointed registered Official Calculators to undertake this work at a set price per calculation, until the advent of the modern computor. The Royal National Homing Union, at The Reddings, Nr. Cheltenham, Gloucestershire, installed its own computor and now processes race distances for its members, in fact, a new Rule in the Union Rule Book requires all race distances to be processed by computor, completely barring any future use of the human calculating brain. This means that pigeon racing is a highly progressive sport when compared to almost all others.

When the beginner applies to his local pigeon racing club for membership (please remember that no club affiliated to the Union is bound to accept any application for membership and that it has the power to reject) and is accepted the Secretary accompanied by a member of the club's Management Committee will call on the newly accepted member and produce the club's Ordnance Map. Firstly, they will find the new member's residence on the map and then proceed to find the exact spot in his back garden on which his loft has been erected. Having found the exact site they will pierce the map with a pin, making a perforation exactly on the loft's site. The map is then turned over and a small circle is drawn round the perforation. The beginner's name is then written beside the circle.

This Ordnance Map is then sent to the Official Calculator who accurately measures the loft's position and accords to it a Longtitude and Latitude reading. These readings are then referred to the computor which speedily turns out the member's race distances, calculated in miles and yards, to the exact yard from racepoint to loft.

Thus, one half of the problem, that of geography and its mathematics, has been dealt with. Having disposed of distance we must now tackle the problem of Time. In another chapter I have dealt with 'race-marking,' a term which survives from the pioneering days of pigeon racing when a bird's wing was actually ink-stamped with a 'race mark' (number and/or letter) for the purposes of indentification after the race had been flown. Later, rubber race rings, each bearing a visible serial number and a further, 'secret' serial number hidden by the fold in the ring, were introduced to replace the 'race-mark' but because tradition dies hard the race-ringing of racing pigeons is still referred to as the 'race-marking' (done at the Marking Station).

When a pigeon is being 'race-rung' a rubber ring is placed on the four spokes of a specially designed 'ringing machine' which when manually operated expands the ring by stretching it. The bird's claw is then thrust through the centre of the expanded ring which, when another lever is depressed, shoots off the four prongs to encircle the bird's leg. When the bird returns to its home loft it is its owner's responsibility to remove the race rubber from his bird's leg, place it in a metal or plastic 'spool' or 'thimble', drop the 'spool' into his automatic timing clock and by operating its handle, or lever, cause the internal printing mechanism to record the bird's time of arrival.

The vitally necessary timing clock is specially designed to perform four main and related operations (1) It must contain an 8-day continuously running clock mechanism of great reliability and very robust construction. On the spindles which turn will be mounted four printing-hands to record the passing of Days, Hours, Minutes and Seconds. These printing hands will turn inside the fixed and embossed dial calibrations. (2) An automatic independent printing mechanism fired by a reciprocating spring which in conjunction with an inked ribbon impinges on the calibrations and printing hands to record four printed clock dials and hand indicators on a paper ribbon. (3) A spool carrier and indexor which automatically moves the spool carrier away from the timing aperture and carries it to an indexed station. Incidentally, the paper ribbon also moves to bring a plain unprinted portion of the ribbon to stand before the printing dials, ready for a further imprinting.

(4) A self-locking case fitted with strike mechanism which is unfakeable and so designed that the time recording mechanism and the timepiece itself cannot be tampered with, or manipulated in anyway, after the club's Official Clock Setter has wound, set and sealed the clock and case.

Before the members may take possession of their clock the Clock Setter will wind the 8-day mainspring and set the printing hands of the clock to accord with the exact time, to the second, of the club's Master Timer. He will load a paper roll into the clock, set the Spool Carrier so that it receives the first 'spool' in the Spool Carrier's Number One hole, or drawer, before closing the clock case and sealing it. The timer is then handed to its owner who is responsible for returning it, after the race, by the stipulated time.

Before any move can be made to calculate a pigeon's flying velocity two problems must be solved. Note that the Union Rule states that the result of the race must be decided by 'Velocity proper'. In other words, the bird making the greatest number of yards per minute over the course is the winner.

The Conveyer/Liberator will notify the organisation of the exact time at which he tossed the birds. What the officials must calculate and decide on is how much time elapsed between time of liberation and the time actually recorded on the member's timer.

Firstly, the officials check what is termed 'The Long Run'. This term means the amount of time the clock has been running since it was set and 'struck off' on the Friday evening at, say, 7 p.m., and the time on the Saturday evening, say, 7 p.m. when it was struck off, both strikes having been made by Master Timer. 'The Long Run' will confirm one of two things, viz. that the timepiece has either gained or lost a margin of time over the 24 hours of its 'Long Run'. Let us assume that the timer gained 48 seconds over the 'Long Run' which is equal to 2 seconds per hour over 24 hours.

Having discovered the 'clock variation' – as it is called – we must relate it to the 'Short Run' which is the amount of time the clock ran from the time the birds were liberated at the racepoint until the time of 'clocking' the bird. It is necessary to calculate the short run because it would manifestly be unfair to deduct the whole of the 48 seconds time gain from the long run. We are concerned only with the clock's variation during the actual period of the race. Time which passed before and since has no positive influence on the race. Therefore, if we find that the race was of 3 hours duration we deduct 6 seconds from the recorded time in order to produce the mean figure on which we base the bird's velocity. The mean flying time in hours, minutes and seconds is then processed to produce a figure wholly in seconds.

Our final calculation is to divide the distance by the flying time. Therefore, we take the member's distance in miles and yards and reduce it first to yards and then, by multiplication, to 60ths of yards. The resulting figure is then divided by the total flying time in seconds to produce a final figure of 'yards per minute'.

The working out of such a velocity by pen on paper is a laborious venture in long division. In these modern times most pigeon clubs possess their own mechanical or electronic calculators. An electric calculator can process and produce a velocity in about three seconds so that the production of a prize list is no real problem.

Most clubs pay out four cash prizes per race and these are usually calculated on the basis of 40 per cent 1st prize, then 30 per cent, 20 per cent and 10 per cent.

In addition to money prizes members also compete for 'Pools'. (It should be noted that in pigeon racing there is no book-making.) The pool entries range from a few pence to pounds, viz. 6d, 1/–, 2/6, 5/–, 10/– and £1 pools. None of these pools is obligatory. In effect, a member enters one or more birds in one or more pools, according to his fancy of his chances. It is usual for the club to pay out one in twenty in all pools up to 10/– and £1 when it is customary to pay out one in ten. This means that if, say, 120 birds are entered in the 1/– pools then six birds can win 20/– each. Other schemes are also resorted to in an effort to 'spread' prizes, such as 'Nominations', 'Knock Out', 'Snowball', etc. The fact is that no exciting rewards are available at club level. Real incentives appear only at Championship Club, Specialist Club and National 'Open' Event levels. National clubs pay out upwards of £40,000 per race and some even offer motor cars as prizes.

In the main, prize money (as distinct from pools) is extracted from what is known as 'Birdage Fees'. The 'birdage' is the amount of money a member pays to enter a pigeon in a race, an amount which tends to increase according to the increasing distances of the race programme. Naturally, the clubs with the large memberships pay out the greatest amount of prize money but the tendency among fanciers is to splinter the large clubs in favour of promoting many small ones in which membership averages from eight to twenty.

The rules require every member to pay for his own 'race distance calculations' at so-much per distance and any member who moves his loft to another site must pay the cost of re-measurement. A fancier can fly in more than one club and he can fly to more than one loft if he so desires. Some fanciers like to race their birds on both North and South Roads so they join clubs which specialise in one route or the other. This means they need two timers and two teams of racing pigeons. Attempts made by fanciers to make the one team of birds compete on two roads, North to South and South to North at the same time, have not been successful and are not to be recommended.

Anyone who reads this book from cover to cover must consider the proposition that pigeon racing is not merely a sport but an art and a science. A measure of art and of science enters into most sports but into none do they penetrate quite so deeply as in pigeon racing, where they totally govern the practice. Notice, too, that the total elimination of the human element between the time that the birds are tossed at the racepoint, and the actual timing of the birds on their return home, probably makes pigeon racing the most honest and human-error-free sport in the world. No jockey rides the pigeon's back to make it obey its trainer's wishes. Once it is airborne it is free to fly as fast, or as slowly, as it pleases because no whips or spurs can goad it.

The onus is fairly and squarely on the owner to breed good, competitive racing pigeons, to raise and train them properly and through good feeding and the practice of hygiene bring them into that high state of robust good health which they need to attain if they are to triumph in a race. The race is always won by the fittest pigeon who gets the advantage of wind and drag-weight plus that little bit of luck which is inseparable from pigeon racing.

From time to time some fathead who thinks he knows the secret of how to fake his Timing Clock 'has a go'. Of course, he is caught out and suffers the usual penalty of life suspension. In other words, he is 'warned off'. The officials who preside over our sport are very efficient and very experienced fanciers. They know all about 'impossible velocities' and those who achieve them. It is in the natural order of things that fanciers who 'win out of turn' become objects of suspicion. As such they are watched and traps are set. Criminals are soon caught and expelled. What is so remarkable about pigeon racing is the fantastically small percentage of villains in our ranks. If one fancier is caught and expelled every year the average is greatly exceeded. No one has yet succeeded in explaining why pigeon racing, of all sports, attracts the greatest proportion of honest sportsmen. My own opinion rests on grounds that are purely sentimental. I think fanciers develop such a great love of their pigeons that they resist all temptations which involve the risk of losing them. Some races are required to be flown 'on the day'. In others, notably those enacted over very long distances, race-time is extended to cover a number of days. In these events officials recognise the fact that pigeons do not fly at night so they deduct what is termed 'hours of darkness' from the clock's running time (Long Run). In mid-summer, 'hours of darkness' start at ten o'clock in the evening and extend to four o'clock (dawn). The theory that holds that racing pigeons who have roosted for the night necessarily wake and take to the air again at dawn is a pleasing one which is totally without foundation.

Index

anaemia, 69, 90, 93
aviaries, 42, 43

Barker, N., 43
beak: length of, 50; lower mandible, 49; slot, 49
Beaufort Scale of Wind Forces, 18
'bloom', 53, 145, 146, 149
breeding: 'closed season', 59; breeding time, 79; egg-laying period, 73; elimination, 60; 'fallow generation', 63; fertility, 72, 73; from aged pigeons, 51; inbreeding, 56, 66, 67, 70; incubation, 74; line-breeding, 66, 70, 71; Mendelian Law, 60, 64, 65, 70, 71; Outcrossing, 66; ratio of good cocks to hens, 69; sex-linkage, 70, 81
broken leg, treatment, 156–7

Canker *see* Trichmonais
carbohydrates, 86, 89, 94; content of grains, 87
Christopher, Reg, 139, 140

claws, temperature, 46
'closed season', 59
Coccidiosis, 152
conveying, conveyors, 121, 126, 127, 172
crop: crop-bound, 90; Sour Crop, 156

Delmottes, The, 43
Delrez, The, 43
diet, 78, 85–97, 107; 'boost', 96, 97, 107; carbohydrates, 86, 87, 89, 94; cereals, 86, 88, 89; compounded, 68; grit, 96; Legumes, 86, 87, 89; Oil Seeds, 86, 87; protein, 86, 87, 148; Silicon, 86; vitamins, 88, 89, 90, 91
Diseases: Coccidiosis, 152; Escheria Coli, 153, 154; Itch (Depluming) Mite, 27, 258; Liver Fluke, 158; One-Eyed Cold, 154; Pigeon Pox, 154–5; Polyneuritis, 90, 153–4; respiratory disease, 13, 15, 17, 45, 49, 50, 94, 151; 'roup', 27; Trichmonais, 49, 154; tumours, 51

178 INDEX

Drag, The, 101, 121–31; breaking-point, 128, 129; pilot birds, 128

Escheria Coli, 153, 154
Eye, 50; mechanism, 141–2; Nictating membrane, 50
Eye-Sign, 67, 133–43; definition, 142; disappearance at death, 142; Formula of Recognition, 137, 138, 139, 142; Inspection Code, 135, 136; iris colour, 67, 136–7; 'matching', 140

'Fly-Away, The', 14, 106
foundation stock, 39–57; breeding from, 41; choice of, 45 –53; old birds, 41, 42, 44, 55; paper pedigree, 55; pedigree, 54; prisoner stock, 42, 43; squeakers, 40, 41, 44, 55, 67
'Four-Wall Ventilation', 17
fret-marks, 47, 147, 148

Gigot, 134, 137
Gits, The, 43
Gobert, Mons, 133, 137, 138, 139
grain : cereals, 86, 87; Legumes, 86, 87, 148; oil seeds, 86, 87; 'Pigeon Mixtures', 89; Tic Beans, 90, 95
Great Circle System, 170
gregariousness, 109, 126
Grooters, The, 43
Gurnay, Renier, 43, 118

Hansenne, 43, 116, 118
hempseed, 23, 78, 96
hens : affection, 163–4; reproductory system, 163–7
home corridor, 123, 124, 128, 129, 169
homing, 65, 66

Itch (Deplumimg) Mite, 27, 155, 158

Jannsens, The, 43
Jurions, The, 43

keel, bent, 46; deep, 48; in choosing a pigeon, 47, 52; squeakers', 76
keratinization, 146, 147

Lamottes, The, 43
Loft, the, 13–27; design, 21–3; draughts, 14; floor, 19, 20; front corridor, 21, 22, 23, 25, 27; insulation, 25; louvre panels, 16–17, 26; old bird section, 22; overcrowding, 14; size, 14; stock loft section, 22; trapping corridor, 21, 22, 23, 26, 27; ventilation, 13, 14, 17, 18; young bird section, 22
Logan, J. W., 43
Lulhams, The, 43

mating, 32, 111, 164–8; 'mating-up box', 32, 33; process of fertilization, 165; sexual display, 71; time for, 149
Mendelian Law, 60, 64, 65, 70, 81
Mercator's Chart, 170
minerals : calcium, 93, 94; chlorine, 93; iron, 93, 94; manganese, 93; phosphorus,

93; potassium, 93; sodium, 93; sulphur, 93
Monosaccharides, 94
Moult, The, 145–9; Big Moult, 147, 148, 149; 'bloom', 145, 146, 149; sign of health, 145
muscle : great pectoral, 47, 48, 51; lesser pectoral, 47

neck, 50
nest-bowl, 31, 35
nest-boxes, 22, 23, 26; design, 31; property of cock, 72; space, 32; swing-door, 31, 33, 34, 35, 71
North of England Homing Union, 37

old birds : choice of, 41, 45–53; dangers of re-settling, 40; training, 103
'Old Hand' : on breeding, 65, 66, 67; on dilettantes, 59; on drinking-water, 91; on loft-decoration, 27; on loft-ventilation, 15, 17, 18, 161; on testing for roundworm, 157
One-Eyed Cold, 154
overfly, 124–5, 126
Oxygen, 94

panic, 24
parasites, 13, 14, 18, 20, 26, 27; atmosphere for, 19; Cocciworm, 19, 20; Depluming Mite (Itch Mite), 27, 155, 158; lice, 155; Red Mite, 74, 155, 156; Trichmonais (canker germ), 19
pedigree, 54; paper, 55
perches : Big Vee, 22, 30, 31, 32; box perch, 29, 31
Pigeon Pox, 154; symptoms, 155
Pigeon Racing News & Gazette, 15, 134
pinion flight, 46
Polyneuritis, 91, 153–4; symptoms, 91, 153
plumage; 'bloom', 53; colour, 81 (dominant), 81, 84, (intense), 83, 84, (recessive), 81; discoloration, 148; greasy, 53; importance of, 52; mite, 155; quality, 18; 'tight', 54
Pneumatic bone, 47
price of pigeons, 114
primary flights, 46, 53; fretmark, 47, 147, 148; moult, 147; replacing damaged, 147
protein, 86; during breeding, 148; minimum requirement, 87

Race Controller, 122
racing : birdage fee, 173; home corridor, 123, 124, 169, (breaking point), 128, 129; Natural System, 111–16, 118; Official Calculators, 170; Official Clock Setter, 172; old birds, 112, 113, 119; prizes, 173; smash, 115, 126, 128, 129, 130; weather influence, 115, 116; yearlings, 112, 113
ranging, 101, 102, 103, 106; refusal, 102
Red Mite, 74, 155, 156
Reid, John, 140
Respiratory Disease, 13, 15, 17, 45, 94, 151, 161; detection, 50–1

respiratory system, 159–61; exhalation, 160
Rheumatic Fever, 49; signs of previous sufferers, 49
road transporters, 122
Rock Dove, pigeon descent from, 17, 63, 82, 83, 85
'roup' disease, 27
Royal National Homing Union, 37, 122
rump, 48

Secret of Eye-Sign, The, 143
Shaw, Fred, 118
Sion, Robert, 136
Soffles, The, 43
squeakers; feeding, 55, 75; foundation stock, 40, 41, 44, 55, 67; navel, 76; protection against scalping, 72; reluctance to self-feeding, 77; small crops, 76; teaching to drink, 56, 77; wet feeders, 76
Stanhopes, The, 43
Stress Syndrome, 14, 106, 117

tail, 48; coverts, 49 (moult), 147; 'fanning', 48; retrices, 48–9 (discoloration), 49, (moult), 147
timing clock, 37, 38, 122, 171; faking, 174; long run, 172, 175; short run, 172
tossing: first road toss, 104; multiple, 108; number of, 107; single-up, 109, 129, 130
training, 79, 99–100; basket, 38; 'line-of-flight', 103, 106, 110; old birds, 103; ranging, 101, 102, 103, 106; schedule, 99; time to begin, 103; tossing, 104, 107, 108, 109, 129, 130
trapping: corridor, 21, 22, 23, 26, 78; mixture, 23; open-door system, 23
Trichmonais (canker), 154
tumours, 51

Union Rule Book, 37

Vitamins, 88; A, 89, 90, 91, 154; B, 89, 154; B12, 89, 90, 91, 92, 154; C, 89; D, 89, 91, 154; E, 91; G, 91; Oil Soluble groups, 91
water: cleanliness, 36, 90; at end of race, 119; fear of crossing, 129; necessity, 35, 91; precautions against freezing, 36
wattle, 50
Wegges, The, 43
'Widowhood System' of racing, 35
wing: fret-marks, 47, 147, 148; pinion flight, 46; primary flight, 46, 52, 53; 'scanning', 46; secondary flight, 57
Worms, 157